OWN
YOUR
risk

OWN YOUR risk

HOW MID-SIZED COMPANIES CAN
WIN AT THE INSURANCE GAME

– – – – –

BRADLEY D. JOHNSON, CPCU, ARM

Advantage.

Published by Advantage, Charleston, South Carolina.
Member of Advantage Media Group.

ADVANTAGE is a registered trademark, and the Advantage colophon is a trademark of Advantage Media Group, Inc.

Printed in the United States of America.

10 9 8 7 6 5 4 3 2 1

ISBN: 978-1-64225-210-1
LCCN: 2021913068

Cover design by George Stevens.
Layout design by Wesley Strickland.

This publication is designed to provide accurate and authoritative information in regard to the subject matter covered. It is sold with the understanding that the publisher is not engaged in rendering legal, accounting, or other professional services. If legal advice or other expert assistance is required, the services of a competent professional person should be sought.

Advantage Media Group is proud to be a part of the Tree Neutral® program. Tree Neutral offsets the number of trees consumed in the production and printing of this book by taking proactive steps such as planting trees in direct proportion to the number of trees used to print books. To learn more about Tree Neutral, please visit **www.treeneutral.com**.

Advantage Media Group is a publisher of business, self-improvement, and professional development books and online learning. We help entrepreneurs, business leaders, and professionals share their Stories, Passion, and Knowledge to help others Learn & Grow. Do you have a manuscript or book idea that you would like us to consider for publishing? Please visit **advantagefamily.com**.

To Cecil Y. Ray, Chairman of The Wm. Rigg Co., who gave me a chance in this business when I didn't know what I didn't know. A wonderful mentor and a fantastic human being, he was generous, compassionate, brilliant yet humble, and the kind of leader who made a very competitive business fun.

Also, to all my brothers and sisters at The Wm. Rigg Co.: It was a great ride! I wish it had lasted longer.

CONTENTS

ACKNOWLEDGMENTS

O nce I had the idea for this book, I carried it around with me for years, never sure how I could actually get it done. Thank you to Advantage|ForbesBooks for showing me the way and for publishing *Own Your Risk*. Mike Vargo, a freelance writer and editor in Pittsburgh, worked with me remotely on the writing of the book; without him it couldn't have happened.

I would like to acknowledge all of my clients, who often have tolerated more questions than answers from me. Their companies, and the hard-working people in them, make and build the things that make our economy work. It has been an honor and a privilege to serve you over the last thirty-three years.

My parents, Dean and Mardell Johnson, gave me the best start in life imaginable. My wife, children, and stepchildren provide me with the motivation and support that I need to get up every morning with a smile on my face and gratitude in my heart. As a disciple of Jesus Christ, I find my purpose and my peace in His love and grace. And a final acknowledgment goes to the United States Army, a fantastic place to start for a young guy who needed a challenge and had no idea what he wanted to do with his life.

Bradley D. Johnson
Little Rock, Arkansas
brad.johnson@insurica.com
501-819-3280

IT'S NOT ALL ABOUT THE MONEY— BUT LET'S START THERE

This book is about more than saving money on insurance. It is about potentially saving a *lot* of money—by taking a higher-level approach to how you think about, and manage, the risks of doing business.

The result will be a company that is managed more efficiently overall. If you want to keep growing, you'll be better equipped for it. As your business expands, you will be able to bank relatively greater amounts as profits or growth capital instead of paying onerous premiums—while worrying less.

None of this is rocket science. The new approach is more sophisticated than just buying insurance, but the basic

By *owning your risk,* you can always chart a course that gives you maximum returns with optimum peace of mind.

principles are simple. Once the light bulb clicks on in your mind (if it isn't already on), this approach will shine through as the most sensible way to go. Which it is.

Experts are available who can tackle the complex details for you. They can also advise you on risk management options. And you'll still save money after paying for their services, because now you are in charge. By *owning your risk*, you can always chart a course that gives you maximum returns with optimum peace of mind.

But everybody wants to know one thing up front. When I say you could save a lot of money, the question is, "Like, how much?" Here is a striking example.

THINKING LIKE AN OWNER: BETTER BY HALF

Our firm provides brokerage and risk consulting services. One of our client firms, a construction contractor, was paying about $1.4 million per year in the aggregate for their workers' compensation, general liability, and automobile liability insurance policies. We helped the company migrate to a system that potentially reduces the cost of equivalent coverage by 40 to 45 percent. That's about $560,000 to $630,000 in savings every year. Year after year after year. How did they do it? First, consider the following key principle they have learned. It's what we call adopting an ownership mentality:

Think like the *owner* of an insurance company, not like the customer of one.

This isn't as baffling as it may sound. Many of us practice it when we're managing personal risks. Do you buy insurance for your smartphone? If you are hard on phones, that may be a good idea—but the typical plan is relatively pricey, and it still leaves deductibles to pay when the phone is damaged or lost. You could skip the insurance and hope for the best. Or, you could try what *Consumer Reports* suggested in an article on the subject:

> **Pay yourself the monthly insurance cost.** Add the cost of a plan each year into an emergency fund ... Then you can use that small cushion if you need to replace or repair your phone.[1]

One could call this a form of self-insurance. It's also thinking and acting like an owner, because you can capture benefits the insurance company would otherwise enjoy. If you make it through an extended time with no "claims," you keep the money you've paid to yourself—all of it. Minor repairs might also be covered more cost effectively by just tapping your fund instead of paying premiums plus deductibles.

Meanwhile, the cash in your emergency fund can be invested. That's what an insurance company would do. Your fund is too small to earn much—it's maybe a couple of hundred dollars, earning low interest in a money market account—but imagine the larger possibilities. Imagine putting, say, hundreds of *thousands* of dollars into instruments that yield a bigger bang per buck.

Our construction contractor is capturing the benefits above, and more. Let me briefly share the backstory, which brings out key points we'll develop further as we go along. The owner/CEO of the construction company is a fine gentleman who's been with our firm for years. Like most entrepreneurs, he started small, only putting enough boots

---

1   Mandy Walker, "Is Smartphone Insurance Worth Buying?" *Consumer Reports*, May 11, 2018, https://www.consumerreports.org/insurance/is-smartphone-insurance-worth-buying/.

and equipment on the ground to handle some local projects in his industry niche. And for quite a while he was happy to use us simply as his insurance broker. We had put him in a guaranteed-cost plan with a major insurer that specialized in his industry, which was a conservative choice but in our view the right choice for his situation at the time.

Small businesses tend to do best with conventional insurance. Like larger firms of their type, they face a broad spectrum of risks. Metalworking injuries can happen in a local machine shop or a "Big Three" auto plant. Both also have to be concerned about fire, theft, vandalism and other sorts of mishaps. The difference is that smaller companies, below a certain threshold, are literally too small to benefit from using alternatives to standard commercial insurance. The reasons are complicated, so for now, think in terms of economies of scale: their annual premiums don't reach the dollar scale that would be needed to get sophisticated about owning their risk. Yet these small outfits have to be sure they cover all the bases risk-wise, so the smart thing to do is just hand off the financial responsibility to an insurance company for a fee.

The arrangement worked well for our small contractor. Business went well, too. The CEO and his team bid smart and worked hard. They put crews in the field who completed tricky projects to spec, reliably. And the company grew.

Naturally, insurance coverage had to grow along with it, and when premiums reached about $1.4 million, it was definitely time to rethink. Any premium you pay to a third-party insurer has to cover more than the cost of your expected future claims—typically, it has to cover about *twice* that amount. A major insurance carrier has major operating expenses. Furthermore, although there are various ways of tailoring insurance plans to each customer, your premiums still reflect average claim volumes across large numbers of customers with risk profiles like yours. Chances are you'll wind up paying for claims filed by others. And if you have no claims of your own, you don't get your money back—it's gone forever.

These practices are neither unfair nor unethical. They are simply features of how an insurance company works. The point is that when you pay such a company to "carry" your financial risk, you're also paying for excess baggage. Therefore, it makes sense to flip the script: to own some of your risk instead of transferring it to a third party.

The construction contractor did this in the most complete form possible. With our help, he joined a "group captive"—a mini insurance company owned jointly by a group of contractors to essentially insure themselves. The operating costs are lower. The premiums that each member company must "pay itself" to protect against expected risks are lower, too, and they're invested while waiting to be used. If our guy's company continues having good claim experience, all the benefits will combine to produce those savings of 40 to 45 percent on the million four, with the money accruing to them as their slice of ownership equity in the captive.

Better still, now that claims come straight out of the company's pocket, the owner has his people tightening up further on safety procedures and damage avoidance. They were already doing a good job in those respects; now they've gone from good to great. And there are multiple benefits to that, beyond saving money. You become a better company, period.

Other customers of our firm have taken steps similar to joining a captive but haven't gone all the way. For example, whereas the construction contractor folded his three major insurance lines into the group captive—workers' comp, general liability, and auto—others have "retained" or owned varying amounts of the risk for only one or two lines of coverage, paying an insurance company to cover the rest.

The paybacks are correspondingly less but can clearly be enough to make the move worthwhile. We would advise any company's leaders to find a spot along the spectrum of risk "ownership" that feels right for them.

A PERSONAL NOTE

As for me, I love the work that I do, because I love my customers and the work that *they* do. They're the midsize construction firms and manufacturers who build and make the things that make our society go. They are tremendously creative. They have to be, because they and their people are putting in utility lines, building hospitals, or grinding out precision goods under challenging and even downright dangerous circumstances—confronting big risks every day to do what needs to be done in our country. If I can help them manage those risks, I feel honored to serve them.

And I mean this sincerely. My background includes more than the thirty years I've worked in the business. It includes the years right after college when I served in the US Army as an airborne ranger with the Second Ranger Battalion (based at Fort Lewis, Washington) and with the First Cavalry Division (based at Fort Hood, Texas), during which I learned a few things that apply to risk management. One is the value of being proactive: Don't wait for dangers to come to you. It's far, far better to find out where they are, then go out and handle them on your terms. Take control. Own them.

But enough of that for now. Please don't think I was a war hero; I wasn't. Perhaps later I will share a military story or two, to get at the business lessons we can draw from them. Right now it's best to tackle a common objection that people have to owning their risk, namely, "I've done fine just buying insurance the regular way. Why try to fix what isn't broke?" Some business owners are determined to stick with that course, and it's not my place to tell them they are wrong. If they're making money and enjoying themselves, how could I?

On the other hand, if you are the least bit open to changing the MO—if you sense that maybe, just maybe, you could turn "doing fine" into "doing better!" by being proactive—the following chapter is for you. It's a deeper, behind-the-scenes dive into risk and insurance, which will show how deeply your intuition is correct.

- - - - - - - - - - -

CHAPTER 1

INSIDE THE INSURANCE WORLD (AND WHY IT CAN PAY TO STEP OUTSIDE IT)

To most people, buying insurance feels like an utterly natural thing to do. Granted, it's an expense and therefore a sort of necessary evil, like taxes. But it is required if you want to undergo the risks of driving a car, getting a mortgage, or starting a business. So you follow what seems to be the smart path of least resistance and buy insurance from an insurance company. They know how to handle the job for you. They'll perform the hocus-pocus behind the curtain, and you won't have to worry.

Allow me to pull the curtain aside. Although valuable work is done back there, I want you to see what your insurance premiums are paying for—as well as what they're *not* paying for. By seeing the complete picture, you can fully grasp the value of the approach that was outlined in the introduction—that is, to take back the job of managing your risk as much as possible. Own it, and prosper.

WHAT YOU PAY AND WHAT YOU GET

Let us assume your company is paying $500,000 in annual premiums. Through a professional brokerage and consulting firm like ours, that figure includes about $50,000 to $60,000 in commission payable to your broker *every year that you renew.* Do you feel like you're getting $50,000 to $60,000 worth of services?

I am guessing you aren't. Each time I do a renewal, I bring out the forms to sign, give the customer the certificates of insurance—and that's about it. I will have done my homework beforehand to review the insurance plan and recommend changes that seem appropriate. And, of course, I'll be on call during the year to help with claims or problems. Still, the recurring 10 percent annual commission (to simplify things, I'm going to use 10 percent as an average, but in actuality different policies pay different amounts) is one of the things that makes insurance an attractive business for me as a broker. In cases where the premiums aren't very high, that built-in 10 percent might even be a reasonable surcharge to you, the customer.

But when you reach the half-million level, the change that I will suggest is this: "Let's look at various alternatives to buying straight insurance. And let's begin by looking at everything your $500,000 pays for, in addition to my $50K commission."

Your premiums must help to cover the insurance company's operating costs, and at big, trusted insurers like the ones our firm works with, those costs are high. They have tens of thousands of employees in locations across the country and worldwide. The CEO alone probably gets a compensation package worth upward of $10 million per year. They have layers of management, plus the best IT systems (they hope) that money can buy, and television advertising and promotion budgets that go way beyond ads on Facebook. Think professional golf tournaments and other major sporting events. On top of all that, a Fortune 500 insurance company will make billions of dollars per year in net profit. It all adds up to a magnificent machine, and it runs on the premiums you pay.

Next, consider how your premiums are calculated. Thanks to their very sophisticated ability to gather nationwide data and use computer models, the actuaries at the insurance company know a lot about companies like yours in your specific industry. They can estimate how many claims you're likely to have, totaling so many dollars, et cetera. But you are only a sample of one, and they don't feel like counting on you to stay fairly close to your projected risk profile. An insurance company with many customers needs to have an overall edge when it comes to probabilities of money flowing this way or that. So they essentially put you in a risk pool with a bunch of customers that look approximately like you. Now the law of averages can work in the company's favor across a large sample, and they set the premiums on that basis.

In short, they're counting on the good risks to subsidize the bad. They use the same principle for writing lines of personal insurance. If you drive safely and live in a solid, well-maintained home, you will be rewarded with relatively low rates for auto and homeowner's coverage. However, you're still in a risk pool with many other people, and every year it is inevitable that some of those people will file big claims for totaled cars or houses destroyed by fire. In some cases the policyholders couldn't have done anything to prevent the loss—although you can bet that in more than one case, they slipped up somehow. There will be people in your pool who aren't as consistently careful or diligent as you are. And the rates are set so that when their luck runs out, when the odds catch up to them, *your* premiums help to pay for the damage done.

Now let's talk about Warren Buffett. His investment strategies are seldom daring but reliably smart. They have made him one of the world's wealthiest persons, and he has bought into a certain industry repeatedly. His Berkshire Hathaway holding company owns parts or all of about *seventy* insurance companies. Why does Warren Buffett love insurance? I believe the main reason is the float: the amount of money taken in as premiums that doesn't have to be paid out in claims until sometime in the future—often, depending on the line of insurance, many years in the future. Invested and managed prudently, the float generates reliable investment income. It's essentially a *banking mechanism.* By riding the float, insurance companies become like banks, earning money on the money that customers put into them in the form of premiums. From the customer's point of view, however, there's an important difference.

The money that you deposit in a bank still belongs to you. You might pay some fees to the bank for handling it, or earn some interest from it, but generally you have a legal right to take out the amount you put in. This is not true of premiums on the lines of insurance you buy for your business. Once you pay the money to the insurance company, it's out of your control. The only way you are entitled to get any of it back is by filing a legitimate claim.

And over the long run, it is very difficult to break even, let alone come out ahead. I want to repeat this in more explicit language to make sure it comes across. Rarely will business customers receive, in claims, amounts of money that come close to reimbursing them fully for the premiums they'll ultimately pay. Even more rarely is it possible to realize a "profit" from claims.

You have little chance of either, because two factors are working against you from the get-go: the structure of the insurance industry, and the total cost of risk. Peeking behind the curtain at each will reveal where you truly stand.

THE STRUCTURE OF THE INSURANCE INDUSTRY

There are times when insurance can look like the best investment you ever made. You've had a streak of unfortunate incidents that would have set you back big time if the insurance company hadn't been as good as its word. Instead, they paid out claims that come to much more than you paid them in premiums over the same period. Such a deal!

What you're seeing is a short-term illusion. Or, more accurately, you're seeing insurance provide the service that it is designed to deliver, which is to carry you through an unexpected rough spot that would be hard to navigate otherwise. The folks at the insurance company picked up the risk you had transferred to them, put it on their backs, and carried you across the bridge of risk to the other side.

But they will expect to collect a toll down the road. Your premiums for future periods will go up. In fact, they will increase in amounts calibrated to recoup the losses the insurance company has incurred, sooner or later.

The insurance industry is not structured to let the customers make money. It's structured so the insurance companies make money.

If you file even more claims, they'll keep going up. If you try switching carriers, that probably won't help, because the new potential insurer will require the details of your past claims history.

The insurance industry is not structured to let the customers make money. It's structured so the insurance companies make money. They're playing a long game, at which they are very skillful because they've been playing it for many years. These days they are armed with data-mining and actuarial methods that give them a further edge, enabling them to balance premiums and payouts in a manner that keeps the odds tilted slightly but assuredly in their favor.

Thinking you can beat these companies at their game is like going to a casino and thinking you will beat the house. Maybe you'll have a hot streak right away. But the more you play, the colder your chances get, as here again the game is structured slightly but assuredly in the house's favor. (Adam Smith once observed that there is a way to *guarantee* you will lose money in a lottery: buy all the tickets.) Granted, some people do manage more than occasional winning streaks at a casino. The house keeps an eye on them and adjusts accordingly. Counting cards at the blackjack table worked for a while, but then the tables in most casinos were set up and monitored either to prevent the tactic—they'd throw you out if they caught you doing it—or to make winning a reasonable sum hardly worth the effort.

There are parallels in the insurance industry. Cheat on claims, and you're liable to get busted. Claim too much too often, honestly or dishonestly, and you may become uninsurable at any reasonable rate. Besides, think of the irony of even hoping to beat the insurance game. Filing a claim means that something bad has happened. Would it feel like winning if more bad things happened? Imagine beating the Triple A road service game by getting a battery jump, a flat-tire fix, and a couple of free tows, all for the cost of an annual membership fee. You will get more than your money's worth financially, but the breakdowns and delays will make for a miserable year of driving.

Furthermore, if you total up the hidden or "indirect" costs of your driving misadventures—being late to work, missing an appointment, losing a day of vacation—you will probably find that you've been a loser financially as well. Which brings us to the second factor working against you in insurance.

THE TOTAL COST OF RISK

It is growing common in both business and daily life to consider the total cost of things. For instance, a smart buyer might shop for a new car not just on the basis of sticker price but by taking into account the total cost of ownership. Unfortunately, many businesspeople don't recognize the total cost of risk. Thinking that insurance covers the cost of an accident is only partly true. There are indirect costs it doesn't cover, and they are substantial.

> Thinking that insurance covers the cost of an accident is only partly true. There are indirect costs it doesn't cover, and they are substantial.

Here's a passage from an article in the trade magazine *Industrial Safety & Hygiene News*. The article is focused on machinery accidents, citing data from sources that include OSHA, the National Safety Council, and various insurance carriers:

> Analysis reveals that the actual total cost of an accident can range from four to ten times the direct cost stated by an insurance company, once indirect costs are factored in. Indirect costs can include such things as workplace disruptions, loss of productivity, brand denigration, [and more] … There is the loss of a worker's time because of the accident, the lost productivity by the machine involved

in the accident being idled or requiring repairs, as well as the other machines further down the production line being shut down. And of course, there is litigation …"[2]

Liability insurance policies cover attorney's fees, but especially in a major lawsuit, other burdens pile up. The owner/CEO and key people will spend time tied up in depositions and legal proceedings. Staff members will be pulled away from their usual work to gather information, answer interrogatories, and so forth. It's literally a brain drain—a diversion of brainpower and person-hours that are needed to keep the business running properly. Moreover, if an accident is reported by TV news, you'll learn that the man who said, "There is no such thing as bad publicity" was wrong. And in the most serious cases, which may involve grave injuries and property damage to people outside the company, the repercussions can be like those that Boeing faced after its jetliner crashes, or restaurant chains after food poisoning incidents: lost sales contracts, or threats to the company's very existence.

Some of our client companies have had to wrestle with these issues. They've been good, well-managed companies with owners who were left wondering why they weren't good enough to avoid causing such grief. Nor does it take a major tragedy to create major indirect costs. They can accumulate over time from smaller accidents and incidents. You may not notice that each one is costing four to ten times the amount of the claim, because the insurance agreement spells out a list of costs that it *will* cover, which seems comprehensive—but in fact it's only the sticker price of risk.

Understanding your total cost of risk is a key step toward owning it and managing it cost effectively. We've helped to guide numerous

---

2   Carrie Halle, "Understanding Direct and Indirect Costs of Machinery Accidents," *Industrial Safety & Hygiene News,* March 11, 2019, https://www.ishn.com/articles/110379-understanding-direct-and-indirect-costs-of-machinery-accidents.

companies through the process. Some have recognized, for example, what safety specialists really mean when they say it pays to invest in preventive measures. I know of cases where the slight cost of an extra work procedure or piece of equipment could have headed off much more costly failures.

By now it should also be clear that purchasing insurance is neither a total solution nor the most cost-effective approach for medium to large businesses. So let's review what we have seen so far and hit some points that will move us forward on the journey.

SUMMARIZING AND LOOKING AHEAD

Insurance definitely has a place in the risk management tool kit. For smaller companies, it is the most convenient and surefire way to cover the *direct costs* of typical business risks. But all companies should be aware of their total costs of risk, including indirect costs, and take steps as needed to prevent or minimize them.

Key new point: Addressing your total cost of risk requires looking at your total enterprise and how it's run. This should involve more than just the department or function responsible for buying insurance. If you are a CFO reading this, get your CEO on board. We're not going to reinvent everything, but we need an enterprise-wide view of issues that in fact affect the enterprise as a whole.

Companies spending premiums of $500,000 or more might be ready to move up to more mature and sophisticated levels of risk manage-

When you transfer risk to an insurance company, you turn over control of money that your company could use more cost effectively to its own benefit.

ment. At this point you should recognize that excess costs are built into your premiums—and that when you transfer risk to an insurance company, you turn over control of money that your company could use more cost effectively to its own benefit.

So, what are the next steps? They were introduced briefly in the introduction to this book. *Let's repeat and summarize the key points here*:

The big mental shift is to begin thinking like the owner of an insurance company instead of like the customer.

To the extent that makes sense for your company, you can begin to retain risks and manage them, rather than transferring them to an insurer for a fee. The more risks you retain, the more money you potentially save.

The ultimate form this takes is forming or joining an insurance company you own either partially or wholly (called a captive) that is designed to "self-insure" your firm against certain risks.

When you do this, you are essentially paying premiums to yourself. They will be lower than equivalent premiums paid to an insurance company because you aren't paying for the big company's overhead costs and profits or helping to subsidize claims paid to other customers. An actuary, hired by the captive, can custom-set your premiums at levels that are cost effective while providing sufficient funds to cover your expected claims.

Within a captive, you also get to invest and earn from the "float" amount held for use in paying claims. Overall, you may reap savings of 40 to 50 percent versus simply buying third-party insurance.

Finally, and this is a very important point: If a captive is too radical a step, you can take gradual or partial steps, such as retaining and self-financing just part of your major insurance lines, so that you'll capture most of the benefits that a captive does without all of the up-front costs. Your savings will be proportionately less, but once you look at the options, the main question may be, "Why wait?" Why leave money on someone else's table when you can put it on yours and start *owning your risk*?

All the rest is details. Here's a preview of chapters to come. Feel free to skip ahead to the ones that interest you most.

Chapter 2, "Enterprise Risk Management," uses examples and stories to walk you through a start-up process that our firm uses with new clients. The purpose is to get an enterprise-wide (i.e., company-wide) understanding of all the risks that your business actually faces so that you can then begin to manage them, organically and systematically.

Chapter 3, "The Total Cost of Risk," will give you a more in-depth look at the subject we've just introduced.

Chapter 4, "Financing Risk," is a sort of buyer's guide to owning your risk. It compares the various approaches you can take for obtaining coverage, along the spectrum from a guaranteed cost plan to joining a group captive, and shows how a company can benefit more by "retaining" or owning progressively greater portions of risk instead of paying an insurance company to handle them.

Chapter 5, "Group Captives," is an inside tour of the type of captive that our firm would recommend to most midsize companies. You'll see the pros, the cons, and why I believe the pros greatly outweigh the cons, provided you are a good candidate for captive membership.

Chapter 6, "Loss Control," describes the single most important leverage point that you can use for bringing down all costs of risk.

Chapter 7, "Experience Modifiers," presents a detailed look at the data that go into computing this number—and, in the process, shows how much a company can save by exercising best-in-class loss control.

Chapter 8, "Working with Claims," is about making sure that you get what you're entitled to once a claim has been filed.

Chapter 9, "Immediate Savings (and More)," offers fifty-one—count 'em, fifty-one!—ways that you can start saving on insurance costs quickly, just by taking simple steps that ought to be part of your normal routine anyway.

Chapter 10, "What a Broker Can Do," wraps up the book. It's mainly about getting maximum value from your relationship with a broker/advisor ... and it ultimately comes back to what *you* can do to serve your company and your customers best.

CHAPTER 2

ENTERPRISE RISK MANAGEMENT

L et's start with a basic question. What is "risk"? Simply stated, it's the possibility of something bad happening. For a more technical definition, try this: risk is exposure to outcomes that deviate from expected or desired outcomes in a negative way. There are mathematical definitions, too.

Your concept of risk may be similar to what a judge once said about pornography. You can't define it precisely, but you know it when you see it. The trouble is, most managers don't *see* all the risks their companies face. And their incomplete picture tends to be fragmented and fuzzy, short of a cohesive understanding that would lead to navigating the risks effectively.

This chapter is a journey into risk management from an enterprise-wide perspective. It outlines a process our firm uses with clients to guide them onto a path of identifying, analyzing, and dealing with the immense variety of business risks. You'll hear stories about clients who achieved stellar results, dodging those devious outcomes, and stories of some who are still reaching for the optimum. I will even tell the cautionary tale of how an experienced expert (me) failed to manage a personal business risk properly.

If you decide to adopt enterprise risk management, which I hope you do, there are advisors from firms like ours who can serve as your guide. They have checklists. They've detected more than a few land mines. The best advisors will help you set up an ongoing risk management system appropriate to your company's needs and wants—rigorous enough to do the job, but not so detailed that the process itself becomes a hassle for you.

RISKS THAT LURK VERSUS COMPANIES THAT WIN

Enterprise risk management is a winner's game. It turns a murky sea of negatives into a field of opportunities for improvement. The goal is to make your company *more risk aware* and thereby managed more smoothly overall. Once you identify the full spectrum of risks that lie in your path, and once you understand the impact each can have, you can game-plan better ways of dealing with all of them. This might include buying insurance differently than you did before—maybe more of some kinds and less of others, for example—and it will surely include taking various other steps.

Most companies have already done a good bit of the work required by addressing their main insurance issues at some level. Taking an enterprise view will expand your thinking from there, so you're aware of more than just the "normal" risks. *The universe of risk is much larger than what you traditionally buy insurance for.* There are risks you'll want to find alternate ways of coping with, either because the insurance does not exist or the coverage you would need is too expensive.

For example? Credit risk is one. Insurance is available for that, but many smaller to midsize companies essentially just try to manage it on the fly. They offer friendly credit terms only to customers they know and trust. If they normally sell on a "net 30" basis, they don't worry much about receivable risk. They're too busy doing business to focus on whether they will be paid.

Usually this isn't terribly risky because most people, most of the time, pay what they owe. However, it may deserve a look in your line of work. For example, small and midsize companies tend not to have a very diversified client base. Their customers are mainly in the same industry sector or geographic area. Are there events that could suddenly interfere with *their* business, pushing your invoices down the list of bills to be paid promptly?

And here's an extreme example. We work with a company that has exactly one client. They do all their work for a public utility in a major city. Think of the consequences of losing the client. There may be a way to self-insure against that risk, but for now the owner is simply living with it. His main form of protection is doing everything he can to keep his sole client happy while counting on the fact that the utility relies on his mission-critical services.

Your firm probably serves multiple clients—perhaps many; perhaps an ever-changing roster of them. Still, one risk to any enterprise is perpetuation risk: threats to your long-term ability to survive. Do you have an anchor client or two who account for a major chunk of revenue? If so, consider what would happen if they went away and how you could hedge against that risk.

Consider, too, that some insurance you buy might not provide all the protection you'll actually need. An internal risk in nearly every organization today is the potential for sexual harassment. That's why employment practices liability insurance, or EPLI, can now be bought at reasonable rates to cover legal expenses if you or someone within the company is charged with harassing employees. But the risks don't stop there. More than once during enterprise risk assessments, we have asked a client company, "What if an employee harasses a customer or other person outside the firm? Are you covered for that?"

> **In dealing with harmful behaviors like sexual harassment, insurance isn't enough. Good companies have—and communicate—a culture of zero tolerance for such behavior.**

Some companies aren't sure. Some think they are covered but in fact don't have the extra insurance required. There are two takeaways here.

It pays to compare the wording of your insurance policies with the realities of what can happen in the course of business. When gaps are identified, you'll want to think about how to close them.

In dealing with harmful behaviors like sexual harassment, insurance isn't enough. Good companies have—and communicate—a culture of zero tolerance for such behavior.

And speaking of culture …

HOW CULTURE SUPPORTS RISK MANAGEMENT

Corporate "culture" is more than a nebulous buzzword. It's a name for the set of standards, both written down and informal, that shape the daily conduct of everyone in the company. If activities like cheating, petty theft, and personal insults are widely tolerated—or, worse yet, encouraged—they are signs of an unhealthy culture. A company of this kind invites all sorts of trouble, from legal proceedings to loss of business. Meanwhile, it does *not* invite good, responsible people to join the firm or stay employed.

An underlying purpose of enterprise risk management is to build a *healthy* culture of *risk awareness and risk reduction.* It starts with understanding that risks are part of life. You can't venture outside your home (or for that matter sit at your home computer) without exposure to a few. So, rather than react to them on a hit-or-miss basis, you take a proactive approach: learn to spot them as they emerge, and have a company-wide inventory of methods for taming their capacity to bite you.

The following sections describe the process I'd recommend. These sections cover the territory in a sequence of increasingly rich views. First comes a quick bird's-eye summary of enterprise risk management. Then we'll tour the basic types or categories of business risk you may encounter and finish with a deeper dive into the risk management process.

ENTERPRISE RISK MANAGEMENT IN BRIEF

The process consists of four basic steps.

1. **Identification**—Step one is identifying all your risks and seeing if you are covered for them in some way. Whether or not you choose to buy insurance for each would be a case-by-case call. But the first necessity is just being aware of all the things that could cause you problems.

2. **Analysis**—This is done on the basis of probability and impact. A high-probability, low-impact risk is very likely to occur, perhaps repeatedly, but does only minor damage. These risks are often viewed as a cost of doing business and

are usually best dealt with by trying to minimize them. (For example, almost any company that carries physical inventory will lose some to spoilage or mishandling. The trick is not to let the losses get out of hand.)

A low-probability, high-impact risk is quite different. Your business probably won't burn to the ground or be wiped out by natural disaster, but you should prepare for the possibility. This is the kind of risk that insurance is good at protecting against, if you buy the insurance properly.

Also, there are *finite* or measurable risks versus *unknowable* risks, meaning those whose impact is hard to gauge. For example, if a company vehicle is stolen or somehow rendered unusable, you can easily determine the replacement cost: that's a finite risk. But if a company driver hits another vehicle, damages and costs will depend on the nature of the collision. If the other vehicle happens to be a bus full of passengers, the damages might only amount to a dent and a bad scare ... or they could be enormous. That's an unknowable risk.

3. **Dealing with Risks**—As we've already seen, there are many alternatives to buying insurance, as well as things it's wise to do *in addition* to buying insurance.

4. **Monitoring, Measuring, and Adjusting**—These are ongoing "maintenance" steps. To reap the benefits of enterprise risk management, you'll want to track how your protective systems are working and make changes as needed.

Keeping these four steps in mind, we'll now begin to see how they can apply to the three major categories of business risk. *Disclaimer*: The categories are arbitrarily drawn, and they're mine. In my experience, they make for the most sensible way of parsing out and getting a handle on the myriad different kinds of risks that can arise.

The tour of the categories will hopscotch around a bit. I would like to mix in real-life examples and make some key points as we proceed. Here we go.

RISK CATEGORY 1—RISKS TO WHAT YOU OWN OR HAVE CONTROL OF

Attention business owners and managers: In case you didn't know, everything under your control is potentially at risk of being damaged, misused, or violated. These things include your physical assets such as buildings, equipment, materials, and vehicles. They may include intellectual assets ranging from patents to databases. And, of course, they include the people who work for you. Although you don't own them, you are responsible for them under workers' comp and other laws.

Right away the picture gets complicated, because threats to your assets can come from outside the firm or inside. The risk that vandals might break into your workplace is an external risk. Internal risks are more insidious, as some of your assets—often, your employees—may threaten other assets. You'll need to both identify these risks and judge their impact in order to manage them well.

Employee theft can be a low-impact risk—for example, when office workers take home pens or notepads—but in some kinds of business, the risk is substantial. We have a client who manufactures bolts. To the casual observer, there wouldn't seem to be much in his operation that is worth stealing. The raw material coming into the factory consists of massive spools of thick steel wire, too big to be swiped easily. Inside the plant are huge machines that straighten out the wire, heat-treat it, shear it to length, and cut the threads and form the bolt heads. As for the finished product, you'd have to steal pallets of bolts and then find a way to fence them.

But one item is small and valuable. The threading machinery uses precision cutting heads made with diamond dust. They need to be replaced as they wear down, at a cost of hundreds of dollars for a little package of three. The package would fit in your pocket, and there is a widespread demand for that type of cutting tool, which means a black market can be lucrative. Over a period of time, an employee stole about $650,000 worth.

Look carefully at every aspect of your business to identify enterprise risk. Sometimes big risks hide in small places!

The employee was prosecuted. And fortunately our client had enough insurance to cover the loss. The moral of the story is this: *Look carefully at every aspect of your business to identify enterprise risk. Sometimes big risks hide in small places!*

Another twist is that risks to employees are also risks to the company. The impact can be severe when a so-called key man or key person is involved. Suppose you have a dynamic sales rep who brings in a big portion of your revenue. If the rep dies, your sales plunge, so you'll want cash to at least get you through the period until you rebuild sales, and key man insurance can do that.

There's also the risk of a key person leaving the firm, and a conventional insurance buy isn't the only way to manage it. I remember a day when I was playing golf with a client. Along with his original business, which he owned and managed, he had a division in another city that was equally big and profitable. On the golf course, I asked him a question that's worth asking yourself when you assess enterprise risk: "*What keeps you up at night?* What is the biggest risk you worry about?"

My client said, "I'll tell you what keeps me awake. Wondering what I would do if I ever lost Jerry." Jerry (not his real name) ran the other division, and ran it extremely well. He didn't have health problems; in fact, he was fit and relatively young, but this made him the kind of executive who might be tempted to chase an opportunity elsewhere. So we used insurance as leverage to help keep him aboard. My client bought for Jerry a cash-value life insurance policy that would pay him millions if he stayed with the company for another twenty or more years. It came with an agreement saying that if he left sooner, he'd receive nothing and the company would be the beneficiary of the accumulated cash value. To add clout, we made sure Jerry's wife knew about the agreement.

A deal like this is called "golden handcuffs," although it's really just an attempt to serve the interests of all concerned. When my client pays premiums on the insurance policy, he is investing in the long-term continuity of his business. When and if Jerry gets the cash value, he'll reap an extra reward for his years of valuable work. As of now he remains happily on board, and the division is going great.

Yet another risk comes up in closely held companies with more than one owner. Let's say you and a friend form a company that you own as partners. If that person dies, you may want to have the money to buy out their portion, so you aren't forced to be in business with your late partner's surviving spouse or next of kin.

Not every company needs to manage all these forms of risk and more. But a smart company tries to identify, and figures out how to manage, every risk that might be relevant to it. The day you learn after the fact that you aren't covered for a big one is a bad day. To conduct a fairly comprehensive search in the realm of "risks to things you own or control," also consider the following:

Risks to intellectual assets. You can buy insurance for patents, copyrights, and other IP. This can include proprietary knowledge, known in the law as "trade secrets," though most are not as glamorous as the one that's often cited as an example, the formula for Coca-Cola (which has not been patented because that would require disclosing it).

Financial risks. If you do business in other countries, currency risk is a real concern, meaning the risk that the country's currency will change value against the US dollar. We've mentioned credit risk. And liquidity risk came to the fore when the COVID-19 shutdowns began. Many businesses that failed had heavy debt and not enough liquid assets to service the debt. (A pertinent question here could be, "What is your cash runway?" In venture investing, the term refers to the amount of time that a nonearning start-up has before it will run out of money.)

COVID-19 brings up the risk of business interruption. Insurance for it is sold to protect your revenue stream in case you're shut down by, say, a natural disaster. Business interruption insurance is popular in hurricane zones like the Texas coast, where I have worked.

To repeat a point made earlier, however, insurance is only one risk management tool. Others exist. For example, a manufacturer could manage business interruption risk in several ways. The company could keep backup machinery (perhaps old but still usable) on hand to replace machines ruined in an interruption, until top-notch new machines are available. It could have manufacturing spread among two or more locations not equally at risk. Or strike an agreement with another firm to pick up its production temporarily if needed.

Insurance against high-impact risk is valuable. Sometimes advance planning is more valuable—either in place of insurance or in addition to it—and it may cost less.

RISK CATEGORY 2—DERIVATIVE RISKS

The risks in this category have to do with your customers, suppliers, and partners. I call them derivative because these risks are borne by you but derive from entities you have a relationship with or depend on.

Every general contractor has subcontractors, and vice versa. The contracts between them delineate who is responsible for what and who pays for damages incurred by whom. Derivative risks may abound. The final section of this chapter will note that contract review is an important part of identifying and managing enterprise risk.

Companies of every kind have suppliers. Maybe your business isn't interrupted by events at your location, but can you keep rolling if a key supplier is interrupted? Do you have standby suppliers in place? Would it be worthwhile to line them up?

Then consider the strange case of Hurricane Rita, in 2005. When she built up in the Gulf of Mexico, she was horrific. She appeared to be headed for Houston. The mayor urged people to evacuate. A mass evacuation ensued, raising havoc and shutting down most businesses. Then, as Rita approached, she took a hard right turn and ravaged areas farther up the coast instead. Businesses interrupted in Houston experienced financial loss but no damages. There was nothing to trigger insurance. Add "government"—in this case, the mayor's office—to the list of related entities that can create derivative risks.

RISK CATEGORY 3—RISKS TO THIRD PARTIES FROM YOUR NEGLIGENCE

These liability risks are among the biggest risks that insurance is designed to take care of. If a trucking company's driver backs into a parked car, the company is responsible, and liability insurance will cover the damages. If a manufactured product fails and injures the user, the maker is usually held responsible, and again, appropriate insurance will pay.

Other forms of coverage may well be advisable for your particular business. Directors and officers (D&O) insurance protects board members and executives against liability for actions they've taken on behalf of the company. If they are sued for doing things deemed negligent or harmful—such as breach of fiduciary duties or giving out misleading information—the insurance pays their legal fees and resulting losses up to the specified amount. A typical policy can also cover the company itself in such cases. D&O is essential for publicly traded companies, which often become targets of shareholder lawsuits, class-action suits, and more. Although it's expensive, D&O insurance could be worthwhile for privately held firms in circumstances where the risks are high.

A related but different kind of coverage is commonly known as professional or malpractice insurance. The more general term is errors and omissions insurance, or E&O. Companies that employ architects, design engineers, and other types of designers are among the candidates for this insurance. Even if they didn't actually build a structure that fails to hold up—or even if they contracted out the manufacturing of a faulty product—they can face liability for errors and omissions in the design.

Environmental insurance (a.k.a. pollution insurance) is important for companies in the oil and gas industries, as well as for those that work with hazardous chemicals or waste. The insurance can be written to cover legal expenses, fines, cleanup costs, and damages to third parties.

Cyber insurance is relatively new but has quickly grown popular for all types of companies. A key point is that cyber risks cut both ways: they can impact your company and affect outsiders, too. In a ransomware attack, for example, you are the principal party at risk. The hackers inject a code that locks you out of your computer files until you pay for the "key" to regain access. But in data breaches, which are more common, attackers try to steal sensitive information about your customers. Then you may have to provide them with monitoring services to guard against criminal use of their identities or financial accounts.

Buying every form of insurance that might be useful can be a financial drain in its own right. Further, as we've seen previously, insurance covers only the direct costs of losses incurred. Indirect costs usually add up to much more. We'll take a close look at them in the next chapter on total cost of risk. For now, nearly everything I've described underscores the need to go well beyond buying insurance. In the cyber realm, employees should truly grasp that unsafe personal use of company systems creates security weaknesses that could threaten their livelihood.

And now let's move on to a detailed review of the four-step process for enterprise risk management.

STEP 1: IDENTIFYING RISKS

Your insurance advisor will lead the way through the entire process. Your own people, however, need to play active roles in concert with this person. Involvement of the CEO and ownership is crucial, primarily at the start and then in an oversight capacity. To put it plainly, the company's top leaders must lead. Other key people needed for the process (provided your company has all of these positions) would be the CFO, operations manager, safety specialists, heads of HR and sales, division or department heads—and ultimately all employees.

Risk identification is the first step, although the exact order in which this is done is hard to specify. Often it's an iterative step, as review of documents could prompt a closer physical inspection of some part of the operations, or vice versa. What is important in risk identification is to be as thorough as possible. Typical substeps within the step include the following:

- Covering items on the advisor's checklists.

- Meetings with key officers—and the idea here is not to launch a time-consuming meetingfest. The meetings can range from a select number of formal group sessions to more numerous brief check-ins. All should be highly focused on uncovering potential *action items*—that is, risks that need to be addressed. Sometimes these are turned up by the advisor asking basic interview-type questions. (E.g., "How do you perform this function in your company?" "And if such-and-such happens, what do you do then?") And sometimes a bit of collective brainstorming pays dividends. ("Okay, is there anything we're missing? Joe, Rachel, think about what you've seen on the job. Or what you might've heard about in other companies …")

- Reviews of company records and documents. Financial statements may contain some unusually high expenses, which in turn reflect risky operations. Recurring patterns in the claims history may signal a need for more attention to avoiding certain kinds of accidents. Also, do contracts protect you to the extent they should? Even website and marketing materials should be reviewed—for instance, to see if you are offering performance that can't be safely offered.

- Last on this list but far from least, nothing can substitute for physical inspection. A simple walk-through of the plant or a job site often reveals risks that have gone unnoticed, if it's done with fresh eyes.

You may have seen this phenomenon when a property insurance inspector visits your home. Maybe a tree in the front yard has dead branches about to fall on the roof; maybe the electrical service entrance looks like a fire hazard. Risks can accumulate unnoticed just because you are not constantly searching them out. You're used to seeing the place as it is. You probably keep an eye on things that have caused trouble in the past—"Did the garage door close securely?"—but this very fixation can lead you to miss new forms of trouble waiting to happen.

The same holds true in your workplace. The risk identification process, including keen-eyed physical inspection, is designed to make you more fully risk aware.

STEP 2: RISK ANALYSIS

Once you are aware of your risks, each should be analyzed in terms of two factors:

- How likely is the risk to actually produce an unwanted event?

- How great would the negative impact be on the company's goals and objectives?

You don't have to attempt precise calculations on either count. There is no need in the analysis step for "this type of accident has a 20 percent probability of occurring" or "the accident would cost [insert a figure]." Probability guesstimates can be done by a simple ranking system: low, medium, or high. And while it's important to have a sense of potential cost, dollar estimates can come later—for example, when deciding how much insurance to buy or how much to invest in preventive measures. At this stage it's sufficient to also rank the impact as either low, medium, or high.

The result will be a risk portfolio with various combinations of probability and impact. This allows you to prioritize attention to the risks. You may choose to do little or nothing about the ones rated low probability, low impact: for example, many office workers have cluttered-looking desks, but rarely does the clutter cause serious injury. Unless the person's efficiency suffers, it's no big deal.

At the other end of the spectrum are high-impact risks. They deserve close attention regardless of the probability. You don't want to take a major financial hit or be knocked out of business. The name of the game is to find the most effective, least burdensome way of dealing with these risks.

If you come up with a risk that is judged high probability *and* high impact, it's a screaming red flag. Does it make sense to engage at all in a business process more dangerous than riding a rodeo bull or flying off cliffs in an air suit? A workaround is probably in order. And even low-probability, high-impact risks may call for stern measures if the insurance premiums would be prohibitive. We'll see a dramatic example shortly.

In general, high-impact risks tend to involve liability to third parties. As in the prior example of a collision with a bus full of people, the negative impacts can be *unknowable*—approaching infinity, or, in practical terms, enough to seriously harm your business along with harming others. And generally the best countermeasure to a high-impact risk is to buy as much insurance as you can reasonably afford.

I learned this the hard way in a personal situation some years ago. Although third parties suffered property damages, I wasn't liable for them. The harm that I experienced came right out of my bank account. I own rental houses in the Houston metro area. Since Houston gets hurricanes, I bought flood insurance. One house in particular—a typical three-bedroom, two-bath modern home—carried a rather minimal amount of coverage. It wasn't in a flood plain. The neighborhood had never flooded. Being a risk management guy, though, I figured it was better to be safe than sorry.

Except I wasn't safe enough. Hurricane Harvey brought torrential rains. A levee broke. My rental property was inundated by floodwaters rising *eight feet high*. I rode out in a boat to have a look at it. En route, we gazed down at the rooftops of cars trapped underwater. At the house were two cars belonging to my tenants. They had left the vehicles behind with almost all the rest of their possessions, trusting their insurance to cover the losses. So, after the waters receded, I confronted repairs to the house. It was a wreck. It had to be stripped to the studs and essentially rebuilt; all appliances needed replacing, et cetera. My costs came to $50,000 beyond the insurance coverage.

And here is what stung most. For an extra $50 or $75 per year in premiums, I could have covered that $50,000. Low probability, high impact: I wasn't sufficiently smart to buy as much insurance as I could reasonably afford, and like the shoemaker with holes in his shoes, I had left myself exposed.

Moral of the story: *Think in terms of worst-case scenarios.* Always try to determine the maximum **possible** losses and maximum **probable** losses for each type of risk—right on up to the infinite or "unknowable" level. Don't get caught with a hole in your shoe. Which leads us to the next step of enterprise risk management.

STEP 3: DEALING WITH THE RISKS

To manage enterprise risk effectively, remember a catchy slogan: Quick fixes don't stick. You are out to build a healthier company with a risk-aware culture and reliable mechanisms for controlling risk. This entails having and implementing a *strategy* for each risk you've identified.

Some work up front is required, but before long, you're likely to be saving work and money each year. Instead of patching holes and playing catch-up, you can motor along with systems that are fundamentally risk reductive.

There are times when a single, smart strategic move can eliminate a risk. One of our former clients did this. The client is a gasket manufacturer. The bulk of his business comes from making gaskets that join sections of petroleum pipelines or big pieces of hydraulic equipment. These are critical applications. But in reviewing his contracts, we noticed a line of business that was hypercritical.

He had begun supplying gaskets to aircraft manufacturers. Some of his products were traveling five miles above the ground in commercial jetliners that carried hundreds of people. Jetliner crashes are rare but catastrophic, and therefore they are closely investigated. If one was attributed to a gasket failure—whether the gasket had been correctly installed and maintained or not—it could mean curtains for his company.

We pointed this out to the client. Sales and earnings figures showed the aircraft market to be profitable but not essential to the company's vitality. It was a nice sideline with immense worst-case risk. The trade-off didn't look attractive, and our client exited the business.

And here's a true case in which advance planning trumped insurance coverage. One of my former clients was a company making frozen desserts: cakes, pies, and so forth, all stored in freezers and sold to big-box retail chains, which then sold them to consumers. The retail chains demand rapid delivery, or you won't be selling to them for long. Thus, the client kept plenty of inventory ready to go—close to $15 million worth.

The client's location? As in previous cases, Houston, where Hurricane Ike hit in late summer of 2008. You can imagine what happens to frozen food in south Texas during the warm season when electricity is knocked out. I'd invite you to further imagine how big-box clients would respond if you told them the good news that insurance will cover your losses but you have no supply to provide them. They wouldn't be so happy. They need products in the aisles, and they are counting on yours, which are spoiled.

This worst-case scenario had to be avoided, and there was a simple means of doing so. With our firm's advice, the client had installed generators on site. They were a one-time expense sitting mostly idle until the worst case arrived, when they kicked in. Every cake and pie stayed fresh-frozen. The client didn't lose a dollar's worth of inventory, and he maintained good sales relations with his major clients.

Most risks, unfortunately, can't be managed with a single stroke like shutting down a product line or putting in a generator. They involve calculated judgment calls and follow-up support. If you decide to *transfer* a risk, you can do it the standard way, by purchasing insurance, but even then you'll want safety programs and/or quality control programs that are capable of minimizing claim activity and cutting indirect costs. Some companies, such as construction contractors, can also transfer certain kinds of risk off their shoulders through a variety of hold-harmless and indemnity agreements.

Then there are risks that you choose to *retain* or "own." Several options present themselves. You can self-insure by joining a captive, or by other methods, as later chapters of this book will explain. You can invest in protective mechanisms similar to, though perhaps not as simple as, the food company's on-site electric power plant. You can alter business processes to reduce (if not eliminate) particular risks. Most probably, your company will settle on a strategy that combines transferred and owned risks, in a mixture that looks best suited to your needs and budget.

From there it should be a matter of fine-tuning the specifics while sustaining the company-wide momentum you've created.

STEP 4: MONITOR, MEASURE, AND ADJUST

Finally we come to the step (or, more accurately, set of steps) that never ends. Management of a business is an ongoing process, and you're now making enterprise risk management an integral component. The systems and procedures you adopt may need to be spelled out and explained to people throughout the company at first, especially if they differ greatly from what you were doing before. But many will be familiar, and eventually they should all become second nature.

Monitoring and measuring simply means tracking how well your risk management methods are working. *Adjusting* means bringing the operation more firmly on track. I can't provide a complete instruction manual in this chapter, partly for reasons of space and partly because you wouldn't find it very useful. What you do will be tailored to your organization anyway. But here are some typical key parts of the final, ongoing step:

Audit and analyze continually kept records, which include safety reports, financial statements, claims history, and other insurance information. Delving into the details of each would make a book in itself. Suffice it to say that by monitoring and cross-checking these ongoing records, you gain an enterprise-wide composite picture. The picture should highlight risks that are being controlled cost effectively and those that haven't yet been tamed.

Benchmark yourself against best practices. Your risk advisor can help with this. A person with broad knowledge of your industry, from a risk perspective, knows the latest practices found to reduce risks and costs. If you wish, that person can run an audit showing where you meet the standards and where you fall short. Then you can decide on steps to close the gaps.

Arm your people with the information they'll need. Your claims person needs info and documents to support the claims you file; appropriate parties need information to contest claims filed against the company. This is another case in which you don't want to be caught with a hole in your shoe. It is also important that your key people understand—and, when needed, question—information developed and used by insurance companies. For example, insurance inspectors investigating a claim will set a reserve amount, meaning the sum that the claim is expected to cost. You want reserves to be set high enough that they'll cover the claims, but not higher than necessary, since a history of high reserves will affect your "experience rating" with the company and drive up the premiums you are charged in the future. Bottom lines here: Details matter. Communication makes a difference!

Ongoing inspections are essential. The enterprise risk management process should give your safety people an expanded, renewed awareness of risks to watch for. Now it's their job to exercise this awareness—and to communicate what they're seeing to frontline workers and management alike.

When you do have an accident, **investigate** to learn what went wrong and why. Then you can see how to make a lasting fix—one that reduces the chances of the same thing happening again. Together, inspections and investigation help to make your company a "learning organization"—another example of a term that's more than a nifty buzzword. It's a name for a company that keeps getting better all the time.

Finally, *training makes a big difference* in risk management. The training you need depends on where your people stand currently. What no company can afford is to let inadequately trained people handle risky tasks. The odds of making costly mistakes increase. The mistakes are less defensible. Work processes are slowed down. Employees may grow frustrated and angry. Eventually, so may your customers.

Those last statements describe a company performing below its potential. You and your people deserve a much brighter future. And your chances of building it will grow once you build enterprise risk management into your management tool kit.

- - - - - - - - - - - - -

CHAPTER 3

THE TOTAL COST OF RISK

I t happens every day across the country. Countless small businesses buy their supplies at retail, on an as-needed basis. Somebody from a tiny local ad agency or law firm runs out to buy printer cartridges at a store like Staples. A one-truck residential contractor swings by Lowe's or a nearby lumberyard to pick up materials for the day's job.

When a business of this type grows, it needs to get more sophisticated about procurement. Eventually there will be a manager who takes the longer-term big picture into account, buys at bulk rates, sets up supply chains with fallback suppliers, and so forth. That comprehensive, plan-in-advance approach is the only way to keep the company running smoothly—and it saves a lot of money.

Unfortunately, too many midsize companies neglect to take a similar approach to risk. Their key people continue dealing with it as they did when the business was small. The only cost figures they pay much attention to are this year's insurance premiums, plus direct out-of-pocket expenses such as deductibles. They're rowing hard but missing the big boat—and probably *losing* a lot of money in ways they hadn't recognized.

In the previous chapter on enterprise risk management, we saw that a key step toward "owning your risk" is simply becoming aware of all the potential risks your company may face. Now it's time to get at least a ballpark handle on your true total cost of risk.

If you have not done this before, I can guarantee that the total cost is much higher than you thought, and you don't need to take my word for it. We will look at industry-wide research by respected third parties to help make the case. Further, my intent is more than just to make you say, "Oh my gosh, we're wasting money." The exercise serves a positive purpose.

Once you develop a feel for your total cost of risk—including the so-called hidden costs—you will have both the motivation and the knowledge needed to start cutting those costs. At the end of this chapter, we'll highlight a key leverage point for overall cost reduction.

But there are many helpful steps your company can take, once you recognize the various costs that add up to total cost. *Any company that has grown to the stage of paying a half million to a couple of million dollars per year in insurance premiums* would be advised to trace all of them. Let's proceed with a big-picture review.

THE FORMULA

I can offer a simple formula for estimating the total cost of risk. If you would like to use it for a rough calculation of your total, please do so. Just keep in mind that your records may not give you a dollar figure, or even an approximation, for several costs. Where possible I'll provide a source that helps you plug in proxy numbers.

More accurate accounting can come later. The important takeaway, for now, is just developing an overall grasp of the magnitude of the issue. Here is the formula:

$$
\begin{array}{l}
\text{Insurance Costs} \\
+ \;\; \text{Direct Losses} \\
+ \;\; \text{Indirect Losses} \\
+ \;\; \text{Administrative Costs} \\
\hline
= \;\; \text{TOTAL COST of Risk}
\end{array}
$$

Of course, the picture isn't quite as simple as it looks here. Each of the four cost categories has line items within it. Also, many items are interrelated. When *a* or *b* goes up, *c* or *d* may also go up, and vice versa. It can be daunting to try to wrap your head around all the moving parts. And not surprisingly, some companies never try. We can do better. By going systematically through the items in each category, we can gain a clearer sense of the components and connections that add up to the total cost of risk.

INSURANCE COSTS

These are the most obvious costs. They include the following:

- Premiums that you pay

- Taxes on premiums, where applicable

- Letters of credit, where required

The premiums you pay are fixed for the present moment in time. In a guaranteed cost plan, the rates are fixed for the life of the policy, regardless of how many claims you file. But two facts are crucial to remember.

First, as noted earlier, insurance companies are in business to make money. Your future premiums are subject to change based on your current and past experience, as evidenced by your claim volume. Everyone knows that. The lesser-known part is that your premiums will change by amounts that over time are calculated to let the insurance company make back the money it has paid on claims, with margin to spare. Your future premiums may not reflect an exact dollar-for-dollar correspondence. But neither can you escape the fact that *today's claims will become tomorrow's costs* in the form of premiums paid. Insurance is a mechanism to help you defer and spread out the costs of potential hazards, not avoid them entirely.

> **Your premiums will change by amounts that over time are calculated to let the insurance company make back the money it has paid on claims.**

The second crucial fact is that insurance premiums are only one component of your total cost of risk. High as they are, they probably aren't even the major component. And the **letters of credit** that insurance carriers sometimes require from companies—in order to cover them in case you can't pay—add an extra cost for you, usually around 1 to 3 percent of the credit amount per annum.

DIRECT LOSSES

Direct losses are the kinds that should usually show up on your financial statements as *directly attributable* to risk. They would include the following:

- Deductibles paid on claims

- Out-of-pocket costs for losses not covered by insurance

As for direct **out-of-pocket costs for losses not covered,** ideally you've anticipated those when you identified potential risks company-wide, as described in the chapter on enterprise risk management. And ideally you've dealt with the risks in such a way that the costs are acceptable. If they aren't, it underscores the need to take appropriate steps going forward.

INDIRECT LOSSES

Now we come to a huge and poorly understood category of costs. Indirect losses are "hidden" costs in the sense that they may not be detectable in your financial statements. Many are buried in an assortment of places throughout the financials. For instance, they might be bundled into standard items such as HR costs, production costs, or maintenance and repairs.

However, if you could dig deep enough, you'd find that they are *additional* expenses generated by accidents and claims—and that they've been *inflating* your standard operating costs—probably to the point where their cumulative impact takes a sizable bite out of your bottom line.

OSHA's course materials on workplace accidents state the issue bluntly: "Direct costs are just the tip of the iceberg … What is important to realize is that indirect costs are usually much greater."[3] The amount by which they are greater tends to vary, depending on the nature and severity of the accident. Shortly we'll see a handy estimating tool, but first let's get acquainted with some kinds of indirect costs that commonly arise. An initial list could include the following:[4]

---

3   From "Direct and Indirect Costs of Accidents" by Geigle Safety Group, Inc., in OSHAcademy's Course 700—Introduction to Safety Management, 2019.

4   The list here is a condensed version of the list in OSHA's Course 700, combined with observations the author of this book has made.

Lost production time—When an accident occurs in any type of business, the flow of work comes to a halt. On a construction site or in a factory, work can't resume in the immediate area until injuries and damage are attended to. The problem often ripples to other areas, too, such as when a stoppage in one part of a manufacturing line idles everything. When customers are waiting for finished work, there are costs and consequences to its being delayed.

Makeup costs—Overtime may be needed to make up for lost production. Cleanup and repairs are often needed after an accident. If an employee is injured seriously, you'll have to hire and train a replacement. Further, new hires usually don't perform at peak until they go through a learning curve: You get frequent refrains of "Where do we keep those supplies?" "Oh, I forgot to do X," and so on, which cut into efficiency.

Extra paperwork and administrative time are generated by all of the above. Also, **fines and penalties** typically aren't covered by insurance.

For workers' compensation claims, OSHA provides a web-based tool that estimates typical indirect costs relative to the amount of the claim. You can enter the injury or illness involved—there is a pull-down menu of choices ranging from "concussion," "fracture," and "amputation" to "carpal tunnel syndrome"—and the tool calculates an indirect cost figure. (For instance, expect an "electric shock" accident to create over $130,000 in indirect costs.)[5] Enter your company's profit margin by percent, and it will even tell you the additional sales you'd have to make to gain back the indirect losses.

---

5   The dollar amounts in the estimating tool are based on figures from the National Council on Compensation Insurance (NCCI) for the years 2013–15, and from Stanford University's Department of Civil Engineering Technical Report #260. *Due to ongoing price increases since 2015, today's indirect costs will be higher than shown by the automated estimator.*

As of this book's press time, the calculator is at osha.gov/safe-typays/estimator.html. Or, try searching the title of the OSHA webpage, which is a mouthful: "Estimated Costs of Occupational Injuries and Illnesses and Estimated Impact on a Company's Profitability Worksheet."

But thus far we have talked only about indirect costs related to incidents within the workplace. For a third-party liability incident— where your company has harmed others and/or their property—the indirect costs can skyrocket. Consider just two major types of losses you may face.

Loss of key persons' time in legal proceedings—When third parties are harmed, you can assume they will hire lawyers to sue for damages. And a common practice of the plaintiff's bar, when going after a midsize company, is to barrage the owner and key managers with requests for documents, interrogatories, and depositions. The attorneys know that these people tend to be busy with all sorts of work they can't easily delegate. Therefore, burning their time in legal affairs creates pressure.

Anyone who has been called to a deposition knows the drill. You might spend four to eight hours preparing with your attorney, plus another half day to an entire day at the deposition itself. Then comes the next round of legal obligations, and the next. If you are an owner, you are pulled away from overseeing your company's business. If you are a key manager employed by the company, you're essentially being paid not to do your usual work, while that work gets done in who-knows-what fashion or maybe not at all. Indirect losses of this type can be hard to quantify. Yet there is no doubt that they impose significant costs on the company.

Loss of contracts and/or loss of future sales—I will share a sad story about a client of ours, who owns a contracting firm. One of his crews was doing routine underground work for a local utility. They inadvertently bored through a sewer line, which allowed natural gas to back up into some area homes, resulting in an explosion and a fire. Unfortunately, there were multiple deaths and serious injuries to people living there, along with the loss of a few homes. Clearly this was a tragedy, with the commensurate amount of finger pointing as to who ultimately bore responsibility for the accident. Although it would've been hard for the work crew to avoid the unmarked sewer line and thereby avoid the explosion, they were cast as villains before the accident investigation was even completed. And the public utility, confronting a public relations challenge, chose to end its relationship with my client's firm. The account made up about 30 percent of their business at the time.

Fortunately, cases like this are rare. Your company may never cause such a calamity or experience severe revenue loss *from a single incident.* But the smaller accidents and their indirect costs add up. A document from a major insurer, The Hartford, quoted a study that "found that accidents cost the construction industry about 6.5 percent of the total dollars spent in construction."[6]

And finally, in any accident scenario—whether it involves internal harm, harm to others, or both—there are indirect losses that may be flat-out *impossible* to quantify in dollars. But they are losses in a very real sense. Here are three general kinds.

Negative publicity and damage to reputation—Every negative incident nibbles away at your standing. Even if it isn't covered on TV, remember that we live in the age of social media. Family and friends of injured employees, disgruntled customers, neighbors of

---

6   In "Owner's Responsibility to Construction," a Technical Information Paper by The Hartford Loss Control Department, 2002, https://www.noao.edu/safety/itt_hartford_risk_management_resources/owners_responsiblity_to_construction.pdf.

the company who've had their property damaged—all can spread the word that your company is no good to work for, or no good to do business with. In extreme cases there may be quantifiable dollar costs as well. For embattled clients, we have at various times helped in hiring public relations help, loss-control specialists, independent investigators, and specialized attorneys. The clients paid willingly for these services because the services were *needed*.

Here again, though, it doesn't take a single extreme case to hurt you. Constant low-level streams of negative chatter may actually be worse in some respects. The losses are harder to detect, and countering the bad publicity is a more complex undertaking. The best strategy is preemptive: Don't give people reasons to complain.

Damage to employee morale—To quote a third-party source, "In many instances employee morale suffers, and this usually negatively impacts the quantity and quality of the work they perform. Employee turnover usually increases after a serious accident, and always after a fatality."[7]

Emotional costs to the owner and/or top managers—You've got to be tough just to consider running a company. It is an emotionally demanding life to begin with. An article in *Inc.* magazine puts it this way: Entrepreneurs often juggle many roles and face countless setbacks—lost customers, disputes with partners, increased competition, staffing problems—all while struggling to make payroll. "There are traumatic events all the way along the line," says psychiatrist and former entrepreneur Michael A. Freeman …[8]

Maybe you've moved to a stage at which daily operations go smoother than described here, most of the time. Still,

---

7   As cited earlier, "Direct and Indirect Costs of Accidents" by Geigle Safety Group, for OSHAcademy.

8   Jessica Bruder, "The Psychological Price of Entrepreneurship," *Inc.*, September 2013.

the stresses can take their toll. And in my view, the added grief of knowing that people have suffered grave harm through your company is one of the least recognized burdens of risk.

The contractor in the utility explosion case was deeply affected for years. At one point he confided that he was pondering whether to sell his firm and get out of the industry.

Another client, a structural-steel erector, was on a building site when an employee fell to his death. The company couldn't be blamed for this accident. The deceased had been working only one story above ground and was wearing a fall-protection harness; he'd just made the fatal mistake of not adjusting his safety tie-off to the proper length. The man also happened to be a personal friend of our client, the owner. He told us about rushing to his fallen friend's aid and finding him beyond help. Here again, the initial shock was followed by years of dark reminders and troubling unrest.

We business types usually speak of risk in terms of dollar costs and potential savings. What can't be neglected is the human aspect. A "company," by definition, is a group of *people.* And except for the few who lack basic empathy, all of us who own or manage companies are bound to have personal feelings for the fellow humans we work with.

Several years ago, *Safety+Health* magazine ran an article titled "The ROI of Safety." One person interviewed was the VP of safety for a global manufacturer. That officer, Rich Widdowson of Schneider Electric, duly explained how a particular safety investment at a Schneider plant had "more than paid for itself" through "increased productivity." However, he hesitated to give precise figures:

"I hate to go into the dollar savings. They're there, but that's not why we do it," Widdowson said. "We don't do this because of the dollars. We do this because of the people."[9]

ADMINISTRATIVE COSTS (AND A KEY COST-CONTROL LEVER)

In the equation for total cost of risk, there is one more cost category to consider. It includes the various expenses that your company incurs, routinely, for managing risk. An example would be the administrative costs of filing claims and following through on them. But the most pivotal item in this category is the one we've just mentioned: the cost of your safety program.

Investing in safety gives you leverage for reducing other costs across the board. To the extent that you can cut down on accidents and claims, all other costs of risk are cut accordingly. Future insurance premiums will be lower; direct and indirect losses will be lowered right away.

> To the extent that you can cut down on accidents and claims, all other costs of risk are cut accordingly.

Surely you have been lectured on the subject. Your company's safety record may be better than average. I would urge raising the bar to "*best in class*" better, for the simple reason that it's been proven to pay off time and again. Reliable sources, such as a survey of major-company CFOs by Liberty Mutual, have found that each dollar properly invested in safety can return double the money in savings

---

9   Kyle W. Morrison, "The ROI of Safety," *Safety+Health*, May 23, 2014.

or much more.[10] Big firms like Alcoa have seen profits increase while employee lost time went down when they focused on company-wide safety improvements.[11]

Also consider that whereas some risks and costs are beyond your control, accident prevention is a factor you can influence. This, too, makes it a logical first lever to reach for when you set out to reduce the total cost of risk.

---

10   Liberty Mutual Chief Financial Officer Survey, as cited in "Journey to Safety Excellence: The Business Case for Investment in Safety" from the National Safety Council, 2013.

11   Morrison, "The ROI of Safety," *Safety+Health*, May 23, 2014.

CHAPTER 4

FINANCING RISK

An old joke says that the progress of civilization through the ages has been reflected in three questions. Early humans lived in survival mode:

- "How can we eat?"

- Mastery of food production gave us choices: "What should we eat?"

- And today, many of us ask, "Where shall we dine?"

Credit the British humorist Doug Adams for that. We can apply his setup to the subject of this chapter, as follows:

- Small and early-stage businesses ask, "How can we save a little on insurance?"

- A more advanced question is, "What's our strategy for using insurance?"

- And best, "Where do we stand in terms of owning our risk?"

Insurance is an effective but expensive way of financing risk. It's natural to wonder how you can trim the prices down. But it is hard to trim much, because the arrangement has layers of expense and lost income built into it. You are paying another party—in advance—for the service of covering costs that may or may not arise later, and the other party is able to set the odds in its favor.

Thinking strategically will save you more. As your business grows, you grow aware of the factors that drive up the total cost of risk. You see insurance as just one tool for addressing these factors. And you begin to develop a mixed approach: paying an insurance company to cover some portions of your risk while you self-finance other portions at costs that can be much lower.

This is the path of progression we've talked about in earlier chapters. You are starting to retain or "own" your risk instead of handing it off. Now it's you, not the insurance company, taking control and making choices that move the cost needle in your direction. Then the key question becomes where you can optimize your position on the scale.

Figure 4-1 is a simplified picture of the steps a company can take in financing risk. I'll summarize them briefly, then offer a primer on the considerations that go into choosing each one.

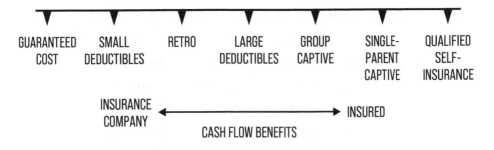

Figure 4-1. Owning your risk: Moving to the right gives you more control and can lower costs.

Most companies start with a **guaranteed cost** insurance plan, paying a flat rate to transfer all their risk to the insurer. Some companies stay there indefinitely. Moving to a plan with **small deductibles**, though, can pay dividends. You get reduced premiums in exchange for taking on a share of the risk. The next possible step, a **retro plan**, is rarely used anymore, but it offers refunds as a reward for low claim volume.

Taking **large deductibles** (say, $50,000 and up) is a serious step toward owning your risk and attacking the costs. Premiums can be reduced dramatically. Your cash flow situation improves significantly. The onus is on you to control claims, since paying the deductibles could eat up your premium savings, so this move requires a strong safety program. Also, there are some detailed decisions to be made in choosing a large-deductible plan that will work optimally for your business. I'll walk you through them shortly, and your own insurance advisor can help with the decision-making.

Joining a **group captive** is the ultimate step for most midsize companies, and it puts you squarely in the ownership seat.

Companies that use large deductibles wisely tend to be very happy with the results.

Joining a **group captive** is the ultimate step for most midsize companies, and it puts you squarely in the ownership seat. You become part of a group of firms pooled together to fund what is essentially a jointly owned, members-only insurance company. This frees you from reliance on the mainstream insurance market. It enables you to minimize costs while capturing the income that big insurers normally earn by investing the premiums you pay them. (Which is why I often describe a captive as a mechanism that "turns insurance from a cost center into a profit center." Although it's unlikely the captive will actually pay you more than you put in, the cost savings and added income go straight to your bottom line in the form of retained earnings in the captive.)

If you truly desire to be on your own, then a **single-parent captive** or **qualified self-insurance** is the answer. Almost no money for the financing of owned risk flows out of your control. You have teams of experts who do everything an insurance company can do, except they do it exclusively to benefit you and your employees and in a manner that you direct. Usually, only large to very large companies use single-parent captives or qualify for self-insurance. But if you are aiming for the Fortune 1000, this is probably how you'll want to finance risk when you arrive.

Finally, please note in figure 4-1 that the **cash flow benefits** go in opposite directions on opposite sides of the scale. At the extreme left, in guaranteed cost plans, insurance companies win the cash flow advantage. They receive the up-front premiums you pay, then get to hold and use your money until it is paid out in the form of claims settlements (and if not paid out, this becomes the insurance company's "profit"). On the extreme right, as just mentioned, self-insurers keep and control their cash for the uses they deem best. Large deductibles and captives bring you progressively closer to this ideal.

KEY POINTS, TOUGH CALLS, AND "ASYMMETRIC WARFARE"

As we zoom in to take a closer look at each form of financing risk, you are sure to see some information you already know. I invite you to keep an eye out for the parts that are news you can use.

And don't be daunted by the fact that making smart choices about risk financing can get complicated. A good independent broker or advisor will help you hack through the weeds. Your roles are to provide data relevant to your company, such as records of your claims history, and to make the final decisions. The broker/advisor should do the heavy work in between: crunching a lot of data, laying out the options available to you, explaining their pros and cons—and, when asked, giving "here's what I would do" advice on key points.

In fact, you *need* such an ally at your side. Anytime you deal with insurance companies, you're in a position somewhat like asymmetric warfare. I don't mean insurance companies are your enemies—they aren't—but they are always armed with superior data and analytic firepower. To the extent that you can equalize the situation, you'll be better off. And the way to do that is with expert guidance grounded in the best information that you and your advisors can assemble.

The sections below are meant to help inform initial thinking. Together they give a bird's-eye overview of what to look for (and what to look out for) when you consider various approaches to financing risk

GUARANTEED COST

Nearly everyone in business is familiar with guaranteed cost plans—or at least thinks they are. A few basics of these plans are well known. They are not loss sensitive, meaning the rates you sign up for can't be raised during the term of the insurance contract in reaction to claims, and a truly guaranteed cost plan doesn't have deductibles, either. So far, so good. You are getting first-dollar coverage at locked-in rates.

However, there is an important distinction that many people miss. If your company grows more than expected during the year—doing a greater volume of business, with more people on the payroll and/or putting more vehicles and equipment into use—you are increasing your "exposures" to risk, and the insurance company will charge you an additional amount to reflect the fact.

It is the same principle that might apply in personal insurance. Suppose you are an unmarried person living alone. Your safe driving record and inexpensive car allow you to buy auto insurance at a nice low rate. Then you meet the person of your dreams, who has a similar driving record and type of car. When you add your partner to the insurance policy, the effective *rate* (per driver and vehicle) may not increase, but you will certainly pay a higher premium.

The same holds true in a guaranteed cost plan, which could more accurately be called a "guaranteed rate plan." All else being equal, a factory that adds employees is more likely to have workplace injuries than before, simply because more people are out on the shop floor doing things. A transportation company that grows its fleet size, putting fifty trucks on the road instead of forty, creates more exposures to risk of an accident. Insurance companies account for this by a formula that goes basically as follows:

Rate × Exposures = Premium

Although the actual calculations are more complex, they determine what you will ultimately pay for a guaranteed cost plan. Your initial quote reflects a *projected* frequency of exposures. For workers' compensation, it's typically based on the expected payroll size and number of hours to be worked during the year. The auto portion will reflect the number and types of vehicles you're expected to use. General liability might be tied to payroll, to sales, or to some other numbers that reflect the volume of business you're projected to do.

You may look at the initial quote and think you've locked in a premium of $500,000, for example, but the insurance company will audit your total exposures. If the final audit shows they've exceeded projections by a factor of 10 percent over the year, you will receive a bill for an additional $50,000.

I am emphasizing this point because many otherwise smart businesspeople are not aware of it. And here is another angle to consider: in cases where exposures decrease, the insurance company will refund money *provided that the contract specifies it.* There are guaranteed cost contracts in which the insurer gets the benefit of the audit if it raises the premium but doesn't have to refund money if the audit goes the other way. The moral is to do more than read the fine print. Ask questions to ensure you truly understand what's being offered.

The moral is to do more than read the fine print. Ask questions to ensure you truly understand what's being offered.

Nonetheless, a guaranteed cost plan is usually the best choice for companies with total premiums from very small to approaching the quarter-million-dollar range. Paying an insurer to take on all of your coverable risk is relatively simple. Once the terms are nailed down to your satisfaction, you can focus on your business. Unless your exposures change significantly, the premium won't change much, and it won't change at all in response to claims. You have handled a year's worth of insurable risk at a price that only changes as exposures change.

The downsides of guaranteed cost have been cited earlier in this book but are worth repeating.

The premium won't be a bargain-basement price. As noted earlier, you are paying for expenses above and beyond the expected cost of claims. You are helping to pay a major insurance company's overhead, which includes the costs of thousands of skilled employees, executive salaries, physical offices, computer systems, advertising, and more. In addition, you are helping to fund claims by other businesses in your risk pool—and on top of everything, the insurance company needs to earn a profit.

You let the insurance company earn money on your money. Investing customers' premium payments until the cash is needed for claims is called earning on the float, and it is a key source of income for insurers.

Your chances of recovering equivalent cash are slim to none. Imagine paying a $250,000 premium for a year in which you file no claims at all. That would be good news in the sense that you've had a perfect safety record while avoiding the indirect costs that come with accidents. The bad news: you're out $250,000.

Nor does it "pay" to have lots of claims. While this year's premium is not loss sensitive, future premiums will reflect your claim experience. *Today's claims become tomorrow's premiums.* Once again, insurance companies are in business to make money, and a high claim volume will raise the rates you are charged in years to come.

Meanwhile, when a company grows to the point where premiums are somewhere between the quarter- and half-million dollar mark per year, it is time to consider moving beyond guaranteed cost. You are now giving away quite a bit of money that could be turned into savings and potential earnings on the cash. And, your claims experience should begin to be extensive enough that your insurance prices can be based on it, more than on that of a larger risk pool.

LOSS-SENSITIVE PLANS WITH SMALL DEDUCTIBLES

Taking a plan with deductibles accomplishes three things right away: it lowers your premium charge, gives use of that cash to you instead of the insurance company, and gives you an immediate financial incentive for reducing claims. Insurance companies generally like deductibles because you are assuming a share of the risk. Indeed, you're paying the initial share, agreeing to reimburse the insurer for the first X dollars paid. On minor claims this may even cover the entire amount.

Deductibles can pay off for you *if you feel good about your safety program* and your ability to minimize claims. Our firm often recommends starting with small deductibles, in the range of thousands of dollars to $10,000. If that goes well, you can quickly move up to larger amounts, which gives you correspondingly greater reductions in premiums.

I'll get deeper into large deductibles shortly, along with some considerations when choosing deductibles of any size. But first, a once-popular type of plan deserves a mention.

ARE RETROS OBSOLETE?

A "retro" plan is retrospectively rated, meaning the premiums themselves are adjusted after the end of the policy period, but they are calculated using actual claims experience. In workers' compensation, for instance, you can earn a partial refund of your premiums if you've been able to reduce injuries, resulting in lower claim costs than what was initially projected. Retros were popular in the 1980s and 1990s, and they can still be good choices in some cases, for reasons that are too detailed to explain here. But they've mostly been phased out by insurance companies in favor of large-deductible programs, which have grown popular because they offer most of the same advantages without the downsides.

LARGE DEDUCTIBLES

By taking large deductibles, you get lower premium costs up front instead of waiting for potential refunds as you would in a retro, and you can save a lot of money overall if you're able to keep claims down. Insurance companies offer premium reductions that encourage high deductibles because it allows them to shed many dollars' worth of risk. A key decision for you—not the only one, but an important one—is just how large a deductible to take on a given line of insurance.

In general, of course, the larger the deductible, the more you save on the premium, although this doesn't necessarily mean to take the biggest deductible you can. A deductible is an owned risk—an obligation to pay when claims come in. Running some numbers for various scenarios will show how the amounts saved on premiums could play out versus projected payments. You'd also want to consider your comfort level with varying degrees of risk. Taking all this into account, with the help of a trusted advisor, should point you toward a sweet spot for your company.

Clients of our firm have chosen deductibles ranging from $50,000 to hundreds of thousands; one went all the way to $1 million. We've had clients choose amounts that looked unusual but in fact made sense for their companies.

One of them, a midsize manufacturer, took a $150,000 deductible on workers' compensation insurance—even though, in nearly twenty years of business, they'd never had a workers' comp claim that high. Their production process consists mostly of sheet-metal fabrication. There are hazards involved, but not the kind that usually pose a risk of catastrophic injury. Most previous claims had amounted to only small fractions of $150,000. The company's leaders calculated that if they could sustain or improve upon their claims record, they would save a sizable sum by pocketing the reduction in premium that came with a $150,000 deductible while in effect paying their own claims.

So far, owning their risk in this fashion has paid off very well. Previously, the company had been on a guaranteed cost plan with annual premiums of around $1 million. In the years since then, the combined cost of premiums plus payments on claims has typically been about *half* that amount or less. And if a serious workplace injury should occur, they are still protected against financial losses above the deductible.

Now let's consider other choices that come up when you go with large deductibles:

- First is the choice of funding mechanism—whether you reimburse the insurance company on a "paid" or "incurred" basis.

- You can also take deductibles on some lines of insurance but not all.

- You can take deductibles per occurrence, or per claim.

- And you can set an aggregate, meaning a cap on the total deductibles for which you are responsible in a given year.

Paid versus incurred—With paid deductibles, you pay the insurance company when it actually pays out money on a claim, as each payment is followed by a bill to you. With incurred deductibles, you cover the entire reserve that the insurance company sets aside for the expected cost of the claim. On some types of claims, the difference may not matter much; on others, the difference to you can be substantial.

Suppose that one of your company's drivers has an accident, causing damage to the other vehicle and injuring the person inside. The insurance adjuster sets the reserve at $100,000. Let's assume this is also the size of your deductible, and if it's an incurred deductible, you will owe the full amount right away.

Your cash flow picture might look much better with a paid deductible. You will be billed for repairs to the vehicle fairly soon, but that charge won't be close to $100,000—say, about $10,000. Meanwhile, the claimant will probably hire a lawyer to sue for medical expenses and compensatory damages related to the injuries. Settlement will take time. It could be quite a while before you have to pay the remaining $90,000.

Why, then, would anyone choose an incurred deductible? One reason is that paid deductibles involve additional costs and hassles. Insurance companies typically require a letter of credit from your bank to help assure they'll be reimbursed. You will pay a fee on the letter of credit. Also, the amount that you are promising to be good for—

just in case you can't pay it from cash on hand—comes out of your credit line. Therefore, you will have less borrowing power available for business needs. Our sheet-metal fabricator didn't want to go down that path. The company has been growing, and their credit line is a resource they could tap for funding future growth. So they went with an incurred deductible, which was the simplest way *not* to fiddle with what's been working for them.

Deductibles on some types of insurance but not all—A number of our clients are contractors who install and repair underground natural gas lines. Although they work cautiously to avoid accidents, the potential losses are high. An explosion or fire could do great harm to many people. After weighing the risks, one contractor decided on a two-pronged approach to general liability insurance.

The company took a large deductible for the portion that covers property damage and bought zero-deductible, first-dollar coverage for bodily injury. Statistics across the industry would tell you that those claims tend to be the highest. There are fatalities, and there are victims who need prolonged treatment for burns. Insurance companies know this. They also know that in cases where claims can run sky high, deductibles become less of a cushion for them, since they may still be left with huge costs to pay after you reimburse them. Therefore, they may not offer generous discounts on the premium for taking those deductibles. When our contractor saw this, he chose accordingly.

Deductibles per claim versus per occurrence—The choice here can be illustrated by a simple example. Imagine you are responsible for an auto accident that injures the driver and three passengers. This is a single occurrence resulting in five claims: one for each of the four people and a fifth for damage to the car. Deductibles per claim will apply individually, whereas a deductible per occurrence will be applied once to everything.

And that is where the simplicity ends. Decision factors can include the kinds of accidents that are likely to happen in your business, the size(s) of deductibles chosen for a given insurance line, the premiums offered for per claim versus per occurrence, and more. Again, a good broker or advisor can help you sort out the best choice.

Do you want an aggregate?—With an aggregate, your total liability for deductibles is capped at an agreed-upon amount. Beyond that, your deductible drops to zero. The deal might look like a no-brainer until you remember that insurance companies are armed with actuarial expertise. For customers who choose aggregates, they will set the premiums higher by amounts that minimize the likelihood of giving away free rides.

Conversely, customers who go without an aggregate get a discount on the premium for taking high-end risk. If you choose that option, don't do it because you are feeling lucky. Do it on the basis of a solid safety program that gives you confidence in your ability to control claims.

And there is a final topic to address in considering plans with large deductibles.

Should you be concerned about conflicts of interest?—Our clients sometimes raise this question. The issue, in a nutshell: Insurance companies have claims adjusters who work *for them*. These individuals set reserve amounts and make other calculations and decisions that affect how money will be spent. When you are on a large-deductible plan, they're deciding how large chunks of *your* money will be spent. Might they be tempted to burn through it more liberally than their own?

My usual answer is this: I wouldn't worry much about the adjuster being negligent of your interests or outright crooked. My experience has been that most insurance companies try hard to see that their employees act as a fiduciary with your money. Insurance is a highly regulated industry with stiff penalties for bad actions, and it is a competitive industry in which customers who are unhappy with how they're treated can switch to another carrier in the future.

What I would pay attention to is assuring that the adjuster's work is *accurate and inclusive of all relevant information*. We all make data-entry errors once in a while. If we're working from outdated or incomplete information without knowing it, we will inadvertently go wrong. Verify that insurance company representatives have received correct information from you, and check their results. This should address your true area of concern.

> **Verify that insurance company representatives have received correct information from you, and check their results.**

And yet, for some people it's hard to escape the unease they feel about the role of the insurance adjuster. Especially given this irony: their premiums are paying the salary of the adjuster … who makes decisions about the deductibles they pay … but who reports to an insurance company, not to them.

The next step frees you from such concerns and dependencies.

GROUP CAPTIVES

When you join a group captive, your money contributes to employing adjusters and other experts who are responsible to the ownership group—of which you are part. Your money does *not* have to pay for big bureaucracies, advertising budgets, or any of a major insurance company's expenses. As a member of a private insurance collective, along with the heads of other companies you can enjoy lower-than-market-rate premiums that are, in effect, paid to yourself, so you capture cash flow benefits and more.

Group captives are explored fully in the next chapter. Here's a quick preview: I would recommend considering such a captive to any client who qualifies and has a sincere interest. I would advise them that joining a group captive is a major step, not to be taken lightly—that is, not in the spirit of "well, I'll try it for a year and see how it goes." While most captives operate on pretty much the same business model, there are differences among them, and finding the right captive for you is important.

Finally, a group captive is like a private club in the sense that there are obligations and practices to be complied with and standards you'll be expected to maintain. But in my view, these things are not onerous. They are done in order to meet legal requirements and to keep the captive healthy. If this sounds like your game, chapter 5 is for you.

SINGLE-PARENT CAPTIVES, QUALIFIED SELF-INSURANCE, AND A FEW WORDS IN CLOSING

Who do the members of the Fortune 1000 use for their insurance? That's a good question, and while I am not sure of the answer, I would suspect that most or all of them either form single-parent captives or become qualified self-insurers. A single-parent captive functions very much like a group captive except it is wholly owned by one company, and that company is the only member. Qualified self-insurance is a step beyond that. If a company meets the requirements set by its state in the US, it can literally cover itself for the specified lines of insurance without needing to set up a separate captive entity. Either way, companies that take these routes "own their risks" pretty thoroughly. They also buy reinsurance to help protect against calamitous losses, just as big insurance companies do.

You do not have to be the size of a corporate giant to form a single-parent captive or be a qualified self-insurer. You would, however, be larger than the typical client companies served by our firm. Qualified self-insurance in particular isn't one of our areas of expertise. If you would like to make inquiries, a good first step might be to contact a trade association of self-insurers in your state or region.

I will close this chapter with a bit more about two forms of financing risk in which my colleagues and I have considerable knowledge: large-deductible plans and group captives. We see either of these as excellent tools for clients currently paying in the range of $500,000 to $2 million in premiums on guaranteed cost plans. Where appropriate—and where the clients are willing—we like to coach and assist them along the road to large deductibles or a group captive.

Which of the two is best depends on the company's characteristics and preferences. Both can give you significant cost reduction, cash flow advantages, and control of your money and risk. A large deductible plan is "easier" in the sense that you don't need to devote nearly as much up-front cost or initial attention to the setup. Joining a captive is a more definitive break away from business as usual, and it does require costs and attention up front—but once you are there, more benefits can be achieved, to greater degrees.

CHAPTER 5

GROUP CAPTIVES

This chapter is a short introduction to captive insurance companies—call it Group Captives 101. Entire books have been written about the subject, if you are interested in reading up on the details. What I am presenting here will prepare you to *inquire* about the details from a knowledgeable advisor or member of a captive, which is a more direct way of learning what matters most to you.

And I hope you will be inspired to make those inquiries. This chapter is also a bit of a sales pitch for group captives. What I'd like to get across more than anything are the many advantages of joining a captive and how they work together for you—when and if you are accepted as a member.

Group captives have a selective admission process. They aren't for everybody, nor do they let just anybody join. That is one reason they work so well. Group captives can be extremely effective at jointly managing risk and driving down the cost of risk, because they are quasi-elite risk pools to begin with. Every member company should be considered a "good risk" devoted to getting better and capturing more of the benefits.

THE BASICS—INCLUDING WHY AND HOW YOU WOULD JOIN

A group captive insurance company is owned and controlled by its members. To boil its essence down to a simple sentence (which isn't easy), it is an entity for group self-insurance. There are many captives of various types and sizes throughout the United States, making it possible to find one that could be a good fit for you.

And what would make you a good fit for a group captive? Companies that want to join, and would likely be successful candidates, should generally have these qualities:

- Current premium payments in the $500,000–$2 million range. This indicates that you have the financial capacity to participate.

- A burning desire to get more for less. Expectations and standards are high in a captive. Your level of commitment should be high.

- Sufficient claims experience and underwriting information so that an actuary can accurately calculate your rates.

- *Good* claims experience, reflecting an ability to mitigate their cost. This will make you an asset to a captive, not a burden.

Describing the different varieties of captives that you might join would only complicate things right now. In order to form a concrete picture—one that conveys what it's like to join and participate—let's pick a typical group captive of the kind that we use. This captive has thirty to forty member companies. It is a "homogeneous" captive, meaning the members are all in the same industry as yours. And it is open to adding a new member.

So, a matchmaking procedure begins. You interview representatives of the captive, and they do the same. To decide whether you qualify, they **thoroughly** examine your company, and I am bolding the term to accentuate how detailed the process is. The captive will want to take a hard look at your financials, your claims history, your safety program, your key managers, et cetera. You will want to do the same for their service providers, their funding mechanisms, their corporate governance mechanisms, and their member profiles.

And when it becomes evident there's a match, you join. You may choose to bring a few lines of insurance into the captive, or only one or two. A client of ours moved in their workers' compensation and general liability but kept their auto insurance on a guaranteed cost plan. Their reasoning was this: the company has a large fleet of vehicles in frequent use, which means a lot of exposures to risk. After running comparative numbers (with our help), they decided the best and safest bet was to stay with guaranteed cost for that particular line of insurance.

But their workers' comp and general liability were lines that showed great potential for getting more for less—that is, equal or improved coverage at significantly lower premiums—plus the ability to capture investment income on the float instead of giving it away to a major insurance company. Those are a couple of the main value propositions that a captive offers. In the previous chapter I mentioned a client who cut his net annual insurance expenses roughly in half by going with a large-deductible plan. It's eminently possible to do at least as well in a captive. And the bottom line for the client we're now discussing is that with two major lines of insurance in a captive and one in the conventional insurance market, his company is positioned to reap the benefits of both worlds.

Your ownership in the captive will return dividends.

Initial costs are involved in joining a captive. You will purchase some stock and put in money to set up a loss fund. As to the size of these costs, the amounts and the particulars can vary so much that I hesitate to quote even a ballpark figure. They certainly aren't prohibitive, and more to the point, these initial costs are *investments*. You can get paybacks.

Your ownership in the captive will return dividends. Your loss fund—which is actually part of a multilayered structure of loss funding (with details too complex and variable to go into here)—will be put to work efficiently in covering your claims and will be invested while it's floating.

In short, the initial costs are where the benefits begin. Now let's look inside the captive for a more complete inventory of the benefits.

HOW CAPTIVES WORK TO YOUR ADVANTAGE

There are treatises that explain the organization and operation of captives on a nuts-and-bolts level. These details can be fascinating. I'm going to skip most of them.

For example, the fact that many captives are legally "domiciled" offshore, in places like the Cayman Islands, doesn't really make much difference to you in terms of the benefits you can capture or the downsides you might experience. It does mean that you (and any top managers you bring with you) will probably want to travel to attend one or more ownership meetings each year. Then again, if at least one of the meetings is scheduled in beautiful places such as the

Caymans or Bermuda—and chances are they will be in interesting locales—you might think of the travel expense as an obligation with benefits included.

But even that is a relatively minor detail. Your focus in considering a captive should be on the aspects that make a significant, positive difference from a business perspective. Here is a walk-through of the major aspects.

The money you put into a captive stays in the captive, working for you. How much difference can this make compared to using regular insurance? Start with a well-known statistic: Out of a typical premium you pay to an insurance company, about 50 to 60 percent goes into "claims load"—that is, it's set aside for paying claims. The other 40 to 50 percent pays for the insurance company's overhead expenses and profit.

Who is earning investment income on the float? You are. Not a major insurance company. Every dollar works for you.

Operating expenses in a captive are much lower. The captive is a much smaller, less bureaucratic, leaner-running organization. Every part of it is dedicated to doing insurance work for you and the small group of members. There's no promotional budget—the rest of the world barely knows that the captive exists—and you do not pay another company's costs of maintaining big headquarter buildings, paying expensive CEO salaries, sponsoring professional golf tournaments, or keeping the New York Stock Exchange happy. Right off the bat, significant parts of the premiums that need to be charged to you are cut away.

Now look at the part that goes to claims load. Who is earning investment income on the float? You are. Not a major insurance company. Every dollar works for you.

A captive gives you CONTROL. I have put "control" in all caps because I, from a viewpoint informed by decades in the industry, consider it to be a fundamental and` far-reaching benefit. Its value includes, but is not limited to, controlling the flows of money.

In a group captive, you (as an owner) have some control over who works for you. The captive manager—the crucial person at the top of the lean staff—is hired by, and answers to, the ownership. Due to the growing popularity of group captives in recent times, a rich talent pool of experienced captive managers has developed, so you have the opportunity to choose a good one who *specializes* in the kind of work your captive needs.

The same holds true down the line. Your manager, for example, will contract for the services of a claims company that does nothing but claims. In a homogeneous captive, where all members are in the same industry, the claims provider can even be one specializing in claims for your industry. Investment management in captives that I am familiar with is done on a contract basis by experts from major investment banks. You have the ability to get A-team services in every regard, all from people who are answerable to you and your co-owners.

A captive controls its own decision-making. If there is a problem to be resolved, an opportunity to be seized, or a procedural policy that needs to be set or altered, it's handled internally. Nobody outside the captive makes your decisions. You get no memos from external parties saying, "Hey, we're going to be doing this way from now on." As long as you stay within the laws of the country you are domiciled in—which, incidentally, can be less onerous than those of the US—every X, Y, and Z is done in a way agreeable to you and your co-owners.

The ups and downs of the mainstream insurance market don't affect you nearly as much, either. You are insulated from them to a large degree. When other people's premiums are going up in a "hard" market, the kind where insurance companies need to charge more to make up for widespread losses they have experienced, your rates within the captive can remain more stable. You are affected only by market forces that may impact you directly, and even then, the captive can decide how to respond.

Control makes differences across the board. In just about every scenario that you can imagine, the members of a group captive are able to focus their resources and thereby control their destiny to a greater degree than customers of the general commercial insurance market.

The very first page of this book stated a fundamental principle—a key to owning your risk and prospering—which I will now repeat:

Think like the *owner* of an insurance company, not like the customer of one.

As a member of a captive, you're always thinking like an owner. Because you are.

A captive enables you to get broader coverages than you otherwise could. When you are a customer of the mainstream insurance market, you have two categories of risks: covered and not covered. Most midsize businesses, somewhere within their operations, face at least one type of risk for which they *wish* they could find insurance coverage. But it's not offered. Or it's not offered in their state. Or it's not affordable.

The problem can be addressed in a captive. You can request a "manuscript" coverage—that is, one written to meet the need. And if the request is reasonable, the likely outcome is this: "So it shall be written, so it shall be done." This is especially likely to be the case if more than one owner/member expresses a need for the coverage.

What you're seeing here is another benefit of existing independently, outside bureaucracy. The terms of engagement can be controlled.

And there is a final major aspect of group captives that may sound weird or even unbusinesslike. In fact, it produces multiple tangible business results.

Captives give you the peer benefits of a "country club" environment. This does not mean that captive members play golf and drink cocktails all day. Such activities are available from time to time, but they are not regarded as mission critical. Think for a moment of some of the more productive features of joining a country club.

Businesspeople join, in part, for the chance to network with their peers. Contacts are made, insights are shared, and lessons are learned. Useful knowledge is propagated. A country club also has a resident pro, maybe several. If playing golf or tennis is important to you, you have an opportunity to raise your game.

Parallel phenomena take hold in a captive. Thanks to the selection process—as well as the self-selection that occurs, when only the highly motivated leaders of high-performing companies step forward to apply—you are in an organization of people who represent your industry's cream of the crop. Everybody is a resident pro. And everybody wants to elevate their game. Including you, and you will.

Country clubs have rules of conduct, along with standards written or unwritten that are upheld by peer pressure. You don't do objectionable things in the dining room that would degrade everyone's experience, and so forth.

Similarly, in a captive the standards and peer pressures are real, and they have positive effects. For example, what is most objectionable in a captive is running up a lot of costly claims. That would definitely degrade everyone's experience, as measured in dollars. People in a captive understand that anyone can have a bad year once in a while. They won't throw you out for it. They will, however, want to know what you plan to do about it to see that it doesn't become a habit.

Let me tell you about a client of ours who joined a captive. The company had a better-than-average safety program already in place. On a scale of 1 to 100, I'd say they were at 75 or a little over—a score that would put them in the top quartile compared to all other companies. This client knew going in that such a performance might only be average or below average by captive standards.

So they ramped up efforts company-wide. Word spread quickly that safety precautions formerly observed on a most-of-the-time basis would now be observed on a zero-tolerance basis. Managers were incentivized with bonuses for fewer accidents and penalties for more. The company took other steps that I am not aware of, because it is not my role to track specific safety measures.

But it is part of our role to track results. This client's results have been spectacular since joining the captive. For example, for the current year and based on prior experience, the company's claims were expected to be over $500,000. I am looking at the actual total for the year. Keeping in mind that the year hasn't ended yet, that this is only one year's experience, and that some claims may well be incurred but not reported yet, the figure I'm seeing has to be taken with a grain of salt. Nonetheless, it is a mighty small grain: $12,100.

There is a word for this. The polite, G-rated one is *wow*.

If the company can sustain this kind of performance in the captive year after year—while it *also* benefits from the premium savings, captured investment income, improved safety culture, and more that I have mentioned—you may begin to see why I say that a captive turns insurance from a cost center into a profit center.

While the company's savings will not exceed the amounts put into the captive (the technically strict definition of a profit center), the financial gains will go straight to the bottom line, raising net profit overall. And there will be further positive ripple effects. The company will be able to invest more in growth. Being a contracting firm, it will be able to bid on contracts at a lower price than previously, perhaps win more, and still come out profitable. Gradually it will forge ahead of competitors who aren't so advantaged.

I believe I have made it clear that we are bullish on group captives.

PARTING WORDS

Group captives have downsides. Mostly, however, they're the kind that are negatives only if you judge them to be so *for your company*. You will leave behind some ways of doing business that are familiar to you and your people. You'll have to attend those ownership meetings and either take on, or delegate, some additional responsibilities that go with being part of the ownership group. Altogether, your administrative costs related to managing risk will increase—maybe a lot—and you will have to trust that the returns outweigh the added expense.

If your claim experience is poor, it could lead to cash calls from the captive. Among the other owners, you won't always get your way; your wishes won't always be granted.

And finally, as I mentioned earlier but maybe didn't state clearly enough to make it register, I would strongly advise anyone to view joining a group captive as a long-term commitment. Certainly for more than a year, ideally for at least five to ten. You are allowed to leave when you want; long-term contracts are not required, but disengagement from a captive is not as simple as changing a conventional insurance plan from one year to the next.

Besides, it will take more than a year for the full benefits to kick in and be realized. But when they do, the results tend to accumulate and grow—investment income, capital in the captive, the ongoing impact of savings that can be spent on one's business instead of on premiums. The work has to be done and the process trusted.

CHAPTER 6

- - - - - - - - - - -

LOSS CONTROL

R isk financing—the process of deciding how, and in which form, you want to arrange for insurance—is an important matter that should be addressed with forethought, but it's an after-the-fact kind of step. The insurance creates a funding mechanism to help cover the costs of recovery from mishaps that have happened, after they've happened.

Loss control is proactive and preventive. In my experience, it is *the single most powerful lever you can use to leverage down ALL of the costs associated with accidents and injuries.* It also serves to reduce the associated grief, hassles, and worries. Furthermore, it's an essential companion to risk financing. Without loss control, no form of insurance can deliver its full benefits.

So, what exactly is this secret weapon I'm calling "loss control"? Simply what we usually call "safety." The two terms are virtually synonymous; they're interchangeable. I am using "loss control" to emphasize that safety actually attempts to control loss—which is a very different mindset from thinking that loss events are uncontrollable.

There are safety specialists who can help you with the many hands-on details of making your company's safety program the best it can be. Our firm employs a few of them, and in my experience they are outstanding professionals who are worth their weight in gold. They come from the industries where their wisdom has been forged in the fires of the real world that our clients live in.

However, my area of expertise is seeing the big picture, based on more than thirty years of experience working with business owners and executives. I've found that the ones who get best-in-class results have a strategic approach grounded in three big-picture principles:

- Think of each accident as if you're paying for it out of pocket. Because ultimately, you are.

- In every decision made by everyone in the company, the choice that prevails has to be the safe choice. When there is conflict between safety and production, safety should win every time.

- And in the final analysis, it's all about culture. Behavior is driven by culture, and culture comes from the top—from leadership.

To flesh out the big picture, let's dig a bit deeper into these principles.

THINK OF EACH ACCIDENT AS IF YOU'RE PAYING FOR IT—BECAUSE YOU ARE

Here, I'm reiterating a point made previously in this book: that the cost of claims ultimately comes out of your pocket. And I am often struck by the doubting Thomas aspect. Many business owners don't really get it until they see the evidence. The next chapter, on experience modifiers, will present a couple of real-life mini case studies showing how claim costs in workers' compensation insurance came back to bite the companies involved. You'll get to that chapter soon enough, but for now I will tell you what happens when I give a similar presentation to my clients.

That's when the light bulb goes on. That's when they realize, *Holy mackerel, the insurance company is not really paying these claims.* We're *paying them. The insurance company just funds them now, up front, and then we reimburse the insurer when our future premiums go up, in some cases for years.* In a sense, it's a sort of hidden charge. You're paying in installments that are bundled into a larger overall figure, the premium.

When people recognize that in one form or another, over the long term, they're going to effectively pay their own claims— that's when they get serious about minimizing them.

As for the indirect costs of dealing with the aftermath of an accident, which drive the cost of each accident even higher—those are hidden, too. Since nobody has a separate line item for "indirect costs of accidents," they get bundled in with various other expenses distributed throughout the company's financial statements. But the upshot is that when people recognize that in one form or another, over the long term, they're going to effectively pay their own claims—that's when they get serious about minimizing them. That's when prioritizing safety stops being a slogan and becomes a reality.

And it all gets back to the main theme we've been talking about: owning your risk. You own it whether you think you do or not, because you pay for it over time. So you might as well take active ownership.

IN EVERY DECISION MADE BY EVERYONE, THE CHOICE THAT WINS SHOULD BE THE SAFE CHOICE

What do people do that causes them to have accidents? All sorts of things, and some accidents are truly unavoidable. Your car is stopped at a red light and a driver plows into you from behind. But the true "unavoidables" are very rare. You can walk through big, sprawling petrochemical plants and see signs saying the workplace has gone hundreds of days, or more than a thousand days, without a lost-time accident. Then you see companies that are much smaller that can't go more than a month or two between accidents. The difference maker is that the petrochemical plant people are much more consistently diligent about avoiding accidents, which leads to actually avoiding them. And, of course, they know the importance of this mindset. They're working in an environment where even a small misstep could literally blow up on them.

Which unfortunately happened in a chemical plant in my region of the country some years ago. A forklift driver was towing a small trailer through the plant. While he was trying to back up and turn around, he accidentally snagged a valve sticking out from a pipe and pulled the assembly loose. Volatile liquid started leaking out. A combustible vapor cloud formed. Apparently, the forklift driver and others nearby made all the right moves. They saw the danger. They evacuated immediately. A control room operator called in emergency teams and tried to isolate the leak. But it blew out of control faster than anyone could respond. Explosions, fires, and structural meltdowns cascaded through the site. By the time the fires were controlled *five days later*, the only good news was that no one had died. Over a dozen workers were injured, one seriously, and the damaged unit of the plant needed months of repair before it could restart.[12]

There are two takeaways we can get from this incident.

The first is that you don't know, in advance, what will cause the next accident; therefore, you can't allow even the small stuff to slide. One out of many thousands of valves in a chemical plant sticking out maybe a little farther than the builders should have let it; a driver backing into an aisle that maybe wasn't the very best place for a back-and-turn—small choices, big consequences. Somewhere in the story of almost every accident, there was at least one point where the safest choice wasn't chosen.

Which ties directly to the second takeaway. When an accident does occur, leadership has to look at it and say, "No, this was not just a case of s—t happens. *There was a story behind it.* The workplace was set up in a particular way, and then certain things were done in a particular sequence, all of which led to the bad outcome. If we had been able to change the story at any one of those points, the accident would not have happened. How do we make sure it doesn't happen again?"

Usually when this question is posed, it gets answered in the form of specific corrective measures. Something is redesigned and rebuilt to be safer, or a new work rule is put in. This helps to prevent a recurrence of the same kind of accident. Many times, however, rules and redesigns aren't sufficient. Various kinds of accidents keep happening—often because the employee, in each case, was confronted with a very difficult decision in which there was *pressure* to make the nonsafe choice.

One of the classic pressures in any workplace is the pressure to get the job done. Production versus safety. And the pressure to produce doesn't necessarily have to come in the form of an explicit command

---

12   US Chemical Safety and Hazard Investigation Board, Case Study #2006-01-I-TX, June 2006.

like "Hurry up and just do it!" People can feel it without being told. They have a sense of duty. They know that the reason they're on the job is to perform the job, and therefore the choice to perform and produce instead of doing the safer thing feels like the right choice at the time.

When the chooser is a charter aircraft pilot, the consequences can be grave. In the "Day the Music Died" crash—the 1959 charter plane accident that killed rock and roll musicians Buddy Holly, Ritchie Valens, and J. P. Richardson—the pilot, who also died, had plenty of flying experience. But he attempted a winter-weather night flight that required instrument skills for which he wasn't fully trained or certified.[13] In the 2020 helicopter crash that killed Kobe Bryant along with everyone on board, the pilot flew in foggy conditions that had grounded other local helicopters and for which his company wasn't certified.[14]

> **The only way to substantially control losses is to create an environment in which people are always strongly inclined to choose safety over production or anything else. That's called building a culture.**

I do not know what went through the minds of these two pilots (or their superiors) before they chose to go ahead with their flights. However, both tragedies appeared to be cases where production won out over safety. Charter pilots often have VIP customers who want to get somewhere promptly. There's a natural desire, if not pressure, to give the customers what they want. It can lead a person to underestimate the risk of giving them what nobody wants.

---

13   Civil Aeronautics Board, Aircraft Accident Report 2-0001, September 23, 1959.

14   Reuters, "Helicopter company in Kobe Bryant crash didn't have certificate to fly in fog," February 2, 2020.

Granted, relatively few unsafe choices have fatal outcomes. Much more often the result is either a minor injury, or an accident somewhere between minor and major, or no accident whatsoever—perhaps because people were lucky. But the minors and midmajors add up. Luck has a tendency to run out. And you do not know in advance who will make a small wrong choice that becomes a tipping point.

The only way to substantially control losses is to create an environment in which people are *always* strongly inclined to choose safety over production or anything else. That's called building a culture.

LOSS CONTROL DEPENDS ON CULTURE, AND CULTURE COMES FROM THE TOP—FROM YOUR LEADERSHIP

Preaching safety doesn't build a culture, at least not in itself. Actions speak louder than words. The first step is for a company's leaders to just get it—to understand and believe that safety beats nonsafety a hundred percent of the time—and then to live the belief. You live it in seemingly small ways, such as not even giving off subtle hints or cues that somebody ought to get the job done despite safety concerns. Those cues will be picked up and acted upon. And you live it in large, obvious ways, such as setting up programs that incentivize safety.

Incentives can take many forms, and consensus on what works best is elusive. For example, some people favor the use of bonuses or prizes to incentivize going for long periods without a claim, while others say not to do it that way because it promotes not turning in claims. If you have different divisions, you can use your accounting system to charge claims against them by allocating the claim costs and premium costs. You can use carrots or sticks, on the individual level or the group level, or some combination of some or all of these. The truth is that what works best will probably depend on the nature of the company—or on you. There are safety professionals who can match your thinking on the subject and put together an incentive program that works the way you want it to.

In short, no one size fits all when it comes to the application methods for building a loss-control culture. But I would close by sharing two fundamental guidelines that I believe must be followed in any company in order to lay a foundation for building out the practical parts.

> **The culture you want to aim for is a culture of commitment to safety, not just compliance with the safety manuals.**

Ronn Lehmann, the nationally known safety guru, speaks of the difference between compliance and commitment. Compliance is following the rules so that you aren't punished. Commitment is doing something because you want to do it and believe that it's good. I have heard Ronn use the example of speed limits versus seat belts. We're compliant with the speed limit when somebody is watching, but when we think we're free and clear, not so much. On the other hand, most people are committed to the seat belt. They buckle up all the time, even when nobody's watching. *The culture you want to aim for is a culture of commitment to safety, not just compliance with the safety manuals.*

And there is a mindset you can drift into as a leader that should be a red flag whenever you sense it in yourself or anyone else. It is that tendency to think of accidents as unavoidable: "Well, they're just going to happen. Part of the cost of doing business, or fate, or whatever." This is a mindset of learned helplessness. It is crippling. It can drag you back into tolerating the frequency of accidents and claims that you've had up until now.

Some people are happy with the frequency they've got. One of our clients, an excellent client, has a prosperous and growing company that chugs along with a somewhat better-than-average safety record. On an academic scale it would probably grade out at a B-minus. Claims are fairly frequent, but the nature of the business is such that nearly all of them, for years, have been for minor injuries like cuts and bruises. The employees seem to be OK with the safety risks. They have good jobs combined with job security, in a company where the norm is to be growing and hiring as opposed to shrinking and shedding. Who am I to say this company should change? But at the same time ...

If your inclination is to aim as high as you can go—by bringing losses down as low as they can go—then I applaud you. Grab that loss-control lever and lean in.

CHAPTER 7

EXPERIENCE MODIFIERS

In order to control losses, it is necessary to look beyond the surface statistics at the numbers behind them. Once you fully understand how those numbers can add up against you—and how they *could* add up in your favor—then you have the grasp you need for shifting the game in the direction you want to go.

Since workers' compensation is a major line of insurance, we'll look into a number that is pivotal in determining your total premium: the experience modifier. The looking that we do will include explaining some basic concepts. This is for the benefit of newcomers as well as for business veterans who think they understand the subject but aren't quite sure. So if you find me saying things you already know, please stay tuned for the parts that might shed new light.

We all know that premiums for personal auto insurance can go up or down in response to your driving record. Safe drivers pay less, and people who have accidents pay more. The same thing happens in workers' comp, driven by the experience modifier.

In its simplest form, the function of workers' compensation insurance is to act as a mechanism to provide businesses a way to finance the cost of employee injuries. Essentially, the insurer funds the claims costs up front, then collects the money back from the business over the future three years through the premium, which is calculated by using a significant adjustment factor: the experience modifier. So, in other words, the future premium is adjusted to reflect the past claims experience of the individual business.

So as I just mentioned, the experience modifier is a number derived from your specific claims history over the previous three **completed** policy years. It's calculated once per year, so it will probably change at least a little each time, as the basis is always the most recent three completed years. And what the experience modifier modifies is the premium you will pay for the upcoming year. It grades you on a curve, compared to other companies in your type of industry. The actuaries set up their data crunching so that the average (or "expected" based on actuarial calculations) experience modifier is 1.0. A score of exactly 1.0 will keep your premium at the base premium specified in your policy. If losses from a bunch of claims drive up your experience modifier to 1.2, you will pay 1.2 times the base premium, or 20 percent more.

The best and safest companies have experience modifiers well below 1.0.

Bring the modifier down to 0.8, and you will pay 20 percent less. That's how it works in a nutshell.

And yet right away, at this simplest level of understanding, there's a key point that many people miss. If your experience modifier is slightly above 1.0, it is tempting to think, "Well, we had a few more claims than average, so our premium will be a little more than average—but we aren't taking much of a hit." The point is, why use the average as a benchmark? Shouldn't *best practices* be the benchmark? The best and safest companies have experience modifiers well below 1.0. By comparing your premium to what you would pay with a modifier in the "best-in-class" range as opposed to the "average" range, you'll see how much you could actually be saving. You may find you are leaving a lot of money on the table—not just a little.

An example of the potential savings will come up shortly. From here we'll be using real-world documents to look at the numbers behind the experience modifier.

INSIDE AN EXPERIENCE RATING REPORT

Modifiers are calculated by NCCI, the National Council on Compensation Insurance, a nonprofit group founded and owned by insurance companies to share payroll, claims, and actuarial data. Each year NCCI sends you a report showing the data they've used to determine your modifier. Figure 7-1 is the main page of a 2017 experience rating report for a real company, with the company's name removed to protect their identity.

WORKERS COMPENSATION EXPERIENCE RATING

Risk Name: Risk ID:

Rating Effective Date: 5/31/2017   Production Date: State:

Eff Date: 5/31/2013   Exp Date: 5/31/2014

Code	ELR	D-Ratio	Payroll	Expected Losses	Exp Prim Losses	Claim Data	IJ	OF	Act Inc Losses	Act Prim Losses
5183	1.42	.41	3,117,935	44,275	18,153	7000913255	04	F	33,193	16,000
5606	.32	.40	567,833	1,817	727	3000913242	05	F	1,285	1,285
6319	1.65	.36	2,574,665	42,482	15,294	5000912470	05	F	2,312	2,312
8227	1.15	.39	196,621	2,261	882	99R0752682	05	F	2,822	2,822
8809	.06	.35	62,400	37	13	3000915897	05	F	9,604	9,604
8810	.06	.39	1,546,211	928	362	1000916174	06	F	3,903	3,903
						NO. 7	06	*	5,342	5,342
Policy Total:			8,065,665	**Subject Premium:**	288,644	**Total Act Inc Losses:**			58,461	

Eff Date: 5/31/2014   Exp Date: 5/31/2015

Code	ELR	D-Ratio	Payroll	Expected Losses	Exp Prim Losses	Claim Data	IJ	OF	Act Inc Losses	Act Prim Losses
5183	1.42	.41	3,743,585	53,159	21,795	7000932128	04	F	52,882	16,000
5606	.32	.40	593,523	1,899	760	4000939910	05	F	604	604
6319	1.65	.36	2,794,155	46,104	16,597	5000932882	05	F	7,197	7,197
8227	1.15	.39	223,234	2,567	1,001	6000955869	05	F	7,722	7,722
8809	.06	.35	62,400	37	13	1000940168	05	F	16,595	16,000
8810	.06	.39	2,070,452	1,242	484	NO. 5	06	*	1,553	1,553
Policy Total:			9,487,349	**Subject Premium:**	317,050	**Total Act Inc Losses:**			86,553	

Eff Date: 5/31/2015   Exp Date: 5/31/2016

Code	ELR	D-Ratio	Payroll	Expected Losses	Exp Prim Losses	Claim Data	IJ	OF	Act Inc Losses	Act Prim Losses
5183	1.42	.41	4,295,853	61,001	25,010	8000990341	06	F	508	508
5606	.32	.40	866,250	2,772	1,109	6000984966	06	F	2,392	2,392
6319	1.65	.36	3,512,822	57,962	20,866	6000973995	06	F	5,263	5,263
8227	1.15	.39	201,359	2,316	903	NO. 12	06	*	7,526	7,526
8809	.06	.35	62,400	37	13					
8810	.06	.39	1,788,200	1,073	418					
Policy Total:			10,726,884	**Subject Premium:**	376,594	**Total Act Inc Losses:**			15,689	

Figure 7-1. One company's rating report

The "Effective Date" at the top means that this modifier takes effect on May 31 of the year 2017. Data from the three previous policy periods are included (2013–14, 2014–15, and 2015–16), and they'll be used to set the experience modifier for the 2017–18 policy year. Now let's delve into what the entries in the tables mean and what they tell us. Using the table at the top, for the 2013–14 year we'll start with the column on the far left and move across. I will ignore hard-to-explain items that aren't crucial to the discussion.

"Code"—Payrolls and expected loss data for the year are broken out by the kinds of work your people do according to the NCCI classification codes. This company has workers in codes 5183 (a plumbing code), 5606 (executive supervisors), and several others. *Potential savings tip:* In your own reports, check that the codes are accurate and appropriate. Some occupations are riskier than others—notice in figure 7-1 that 5183 (plumbing work) has a much higher "ELR" (expected loss rate) than supervisory work—and a wrong code assigned to people in your firm could throw off calculations in a way that costs you money.

"Payroll" shows the total dollars paid to the workers in each code during the year. Given their wage rates, this number reflects the number of workers on the job times the hours worked by each, so payroll is used as a simple proxy for risk exposure. Clearly, for example, fifty people working full time are exposed to more risks than twenty-five people working part time. That's an important variable. We've already seen in chapter 5 that more risk exposure drives up the base premium. But it also gets factored into the modifier, as follows.

"Expected Losses" is the dollar amount of claims that an industry-average company would have given the ELR for the code and a payroll of the size shown. (Indeed, on every line, Expected Losses = ELR × Payroll/$100.)

"Claim Data" shows the identifying number of a claim filed during the year, and "Act. Inc. Losses" means actual incurred losses from the claim.

Overall, the company in this report did a pretty good job safety-wise during the 2013–14 policy year. Total actual incurred losses were less than total expected losses, which results in a credit modifier for the year. Looking down at the other tables in figure 7-1, we see they did similarly well in 2014–15 and *very* well in 2015–16. The expected-versus-actual difference was huge that year. Although I won't show the calculations, which are complicated, the company was rewarded with a low modifier for the year ahead:

	Exp Mod
(J) / (K)	.82

And there is one more detail that's useful to know.

Go back up near the top of figure 7-1 to the table for the 2013–14 policy year. Look at the column on the far right called "Act. Prim. Losses." This stands for actual primary losses. The "Primary" figure is the dollar amount that will be used in calculating the modifier, and on the first line, we see that a rather large "Actual Incurred" loss of $33,193 was reduced to $16,000 for purposes of calculation. The reduction is applied to every claim above $16,000 in order not to penalize a company too much for occasional large claims. Notice that all loss amounts under $16,000 are carried over to the "Primary" column in full.

The experience modifier penalizes frequency of claims more than severity of claims.

This does not mean you can get away with large claims. Their impact will be counted against you in other ways. What it means is that the experience modifier *penalizes frequency of claims more than severity of claims.* Suppose that over a certain period you had eight claims of $4,000 each, for a total of $32,000. In the modifier, they'll count against you approximately *twice* as much as a single large claim of $32,000, since that one is cut to $16,000 for the calculation. And there are logical reasons for emphasizing frequency over severity. As insurance companies see it, frequent accidents, even if minor, may indicate a business where the leaders haven't made safety the top priority. They're likely to keep having those little accidents and run an increased risk of stumbling into the big ones. Probabilities matter. Insurance companies make money by being aware of what the numbers tell them; you can save money by being equally aware.

THE COST OF A HIGH MODIFIER

Next, let's look at a different kind of report on a different real company (figure 7-2). We generated this report at our firm using software[15] that we purchased to help us analyze data on our clients and to show them what we're seeing. The client company has been kept anonymous. Their experience modifier, 1.26, is certainly higher than you'd want, though it's not unusual to see them in this range.

Now look at the money this company left on the table. The current premium, as modified, is over $206,000. With just an average modifier of 1.0 they could've cut the premium down into the $160,000 range, saving more than $42,000. A "perfect" safety record—meaning one with no injuries that need workers' comp coverage and therefore with no claims—would slice the modifier almost in half, to 0.65. So when the best they could do, a modifier of 0.65, is subtracted from their actual modifier of 1.26, the difference is the "controllable" amount of

---

15   The software package is ModMaster.

0.61. In dollar terms, this means that they are leaving $100,014 on the table by not "controlling" their claims. So, as I mentioned above, the difference between where they are and just being "average" translates to $42,629, but I suggest that the real point for comparison is the difference between where they are and where they could be: $100,014. Or, said another way, they are paying almost double what they could be paying! They could save about $100,000—on premium cost alone—in one year. Forgoing this amount of savings is roughly equivalent to rolling a Mercedes S-Class off the edge of a cliff every year.

The same amount might also cover the all-in compensation cost of a first-class safety manager. That person, by leading a rigorous safety program, could then illustrate the point that safety pays for itself—in premium savings alone. But premium cost isn't the only cost of risk.

If you were to estimate the indirect costs that could also be saved by eliminating the accidents … and if you consider that some workers' comp claims are for accidents that involve property or liability claims, too … and that loss records have ongoing effects on the premium in future years … it becomes apparent that getting to zero claims would save a total amount considerably more than $100,000. You're starting to throw Ferraris off the cliff.

Making it through a three-year rating period with no workers' comp claims may seem like quite a reach. But it's a worthwhile stretch goal, and perfection is not necessary to reap major benefits. The previous example showed that a modifier of 0.82 is doable. Applying that to the company in the present example will give you savings of around $72,000 per year. Not enough to buy an S-Class, but how about a Corvette?

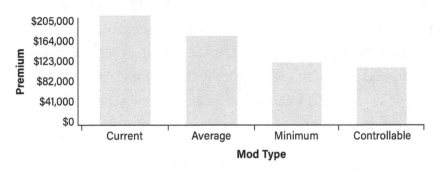

MOD IMPACT ON PREMIUM ANALYSIS

Mod Type	Mod Value	Premium	Description
Current	1.26	$206,586	Your actual mod and estimated premium.
Average	1.00	$163,957	The average mod is always 1.00. This premium represents what the average competitor in your industry is paying.
Minimum	0.65	$106,572	The lowest mod and premium you could achieve if you had zero losses in the experience rating period.
Controllable	0.61	$100,014	The mod points and premium amount you could have saved if you had zero losses in the experience rating period.

Figure 7-2: Profile of a company's actual premium, with savings potential.

HOW CLAIMS IMPACT THE PREMIUM YEAR BY YEAR

We can learn more by digging a bit deeper into the records of the company with a 1.26 modifier. While it's possible to drastically reduce claims from one year to the next, the modifier doesn't go down so rapidly, and neither does the premium. That's because each year's modifier is based on the past *three* years of losses. Which means, for example, that the claims from the most recent year are going to stay in the calculations—and keep impacting the premium—for two more years to come.

There's a constantly rolling carryover effect that can make your head spin. But here are two simple upshots. First, each and every claim, in every year, stays around and keeps raising your premium for three years into the future. And second, when you add up those impacts, they prove that in most cases you really do pay for claims out of your own pocket. Figure 7-3 shows how these phenomena play out for our real-life sample company.

SPECIFIC LOSS SENSITIVITY DETAIL

State	Injury Date	Incurred Loss	Limited / Adjusted Loss	Mod w/o Loss	Impact on Mod	Premium Costs		
						1 yr	2yr	3yr
Itemized Losses								
OK	4/1/2014	$127,122	$127,122	1.1525	0.1098	$18,002	$36,005	$54,007
OK	4/1/2014	$85,388	$85,388	1.1732	0.0891	$14,609	$29,217	$43,826
OK	4/1/2013	$75,676	$75,676	1.1781	0.0842	$13,805	$27,610	$41,416
OK	4/1/2013	$37,719	$37,719	1.1970	0.0653	$10,706	$21,413	$32,119
OK	4/1/2013	$35,461	$35,461	1.1981	0.0642	$10,526	$21,052	$31,578
OK	4/1/2015	$17,672	$17,672	1.2069	0.0554	$18,002	$18,166	$27,250
OK	4/1/2014	$10,596	$10,596	1.2271	0.0352	$9,083	$11,543	$17,314
OK	4/1/2013	$8,701	$8,701	1.2334	0.0289	$5,771	$9,477	$14,215
OK	4/1/2014	$4,895	$4,895	1.2460	0.0163	$4,738	$5,345	$8,017
OK	4/1/2014	$4,084	$4,084	1.2487	0.0136	$2,672	$4,460	$6,689
OK	4/1/2015	$3,631	$3,631	1.2502	0.0121	$2,230	$3,698	$5,952
OK	4/1/2015	$3,464	$3,464	1.2508	0.0115	$1,984	$3,771	$5,657
OK	4/1/2014	$2,304	$2,304	1.2546	0.0077	$1,886	$2,525	$3,787
OK	4/1/2015	$2,304	$2,304	1.2546	0.0077	$1,262	$2,525	$3,787
OK	4/1/2013	$2,154	$646	1.2602	0.0021	$344	$689	$1,033
Grouped Losses								
OK	4/1/2013	$3,020	$906	1.2593	0.0030	$492	$984	$1,476
OK	4/1/2014	$1,736	$521	1.2602	0.0017	$279	$557	$836
OK	4/1/2015	$424	$127	1.2619	0.0004	$66	$131	$197
Grand Totals:		$426,351	$421,217		0.6082	$99,719	$199,437	$299,156

Figure 7-3. Individual claim impacts on future premium payments

What you're seeing is a list of actual workers' comp claims. The "Incurred Loss" column shows the dollar amount that's in the records for each. Skipping to the right a bit, the "Impact on Mod" column shows the contribution that each claim makes to raising the experience modifier. And the next three columns under "Premium Costs" are based on an assumption; namely, that the premium for this company—the base-rate cost that gets modified upward—will stay the same over three years. This is never strictly true, but it's a close approximation. (The average premium used here is the same one we saw in figure 7-2: $163,597.)

So, keeping in mind that the numbers for "Premium Costs" are only estimates, but pretty good estimates, look at the big claim on the first line. It raises the premium by $18,002 per year for three years. The "2yr" and "3yr" columns show the cumulative totals, and by the end of the third year, the company will have paid $54,007 in additional premium costs. They're not paying the entire claim out of pocket—in fact, they're paying less than half of the $127,122 figure in the "Incurred Loss" column—but watch what happens as we move down the list in figure 7-3, through progressively smaller claims.

By the fourth line, where the incurred loss is $37,719, the "3yr" column shows the company paying nearly but not quite the whole claim in added premium costs. And from the sixth line on down, our sample company winds up reimbursing the insurer for *more* than the incurred loss on each claim. Frequency is penalized more than severity.

Skipping to the "Grand Totals" line at the bottom, we find the company paying a cumulative total of almost $300,000 on more than $400,000 worth of incurred losses. The insurer hasn't gotten the customer to pay all of his own claims in full, but don't worry about the insurer. Eventually and by various means (including income from the float), the insurer will come out ahead over the long term.

Meanwhile, from our client company's point of view, there is not much good news in sight. A number of people have been hurt, some of them seriously, while the company paid an extra $299,156 for the privilege of having claims "covered." Their insurance has, essentially, just been a form of credit that finances and defers most of the direct losses. It hasn't covered them in the sense of shielding the company from the costs of those losses. I've said this before, and now you can see it illustrated in black and white.

ISOLATING MAJOR PROBLEM AREAS

The one bright spot in the picture, and it's a potentially important one, is the opportunity to use claims data for identifying and addressing causes of injury. Figure 7-4 is an excerpt from such an analysis done for our sample company. It shows that the most costly single cause is "Strain/Injury from Lifting." Over three years, the company pays about $109,000 in additional premiums for these claims.

> The ultimate takeaway is that digging into the numbers behind your experience modifier can (a) show you how and where you are losing money, and (b) point you to how and where you can save.

Could the money be better spent on prevention? Well, $109,000 will surely buy a couple of forklifts, and probably several if you find a good price. Perhaps that wouldn't eliminate all the lifting injuries, but it could prevent or alleviate some. And the company would have productive equipment for its money instead of spending for no return.

The ultimate takeaway is that digging into the numbers behind your experience modifier can (a) show you how and where you are losing money, and (b) point you to how and where you can save. It's part of a pattern that recurs throughout these chapters. Know your risk so you can own it, and then manage it.

LOSS DETAIL BY CAUSE OF INJURY

State	Injury Date	Claim Number	Incurred Loss	Limited / Adjusted Loss	Impact on Mod	Premium Cost
Cause of Injury: Strain / Injury from - Lifting						
OK	4/1/2014	1319	$127,122	$127,122	0.1098	1 year: $18,002 3 year: $54,007
OK	4/1/2013	1230	$37,719	$37,719	0.0653	1 year: $10,706 3 year: $32,119
OK	4/1/2014	1309	$10,596	$10,596	0.0352	1 year: $5,771 3 year: $17,314
OK	4/1/2015	1483	$3,464	$3,464	0.0115	1 year: $1,886 3 year: $5,657
Subtotals **Number of losses: 4**			**$178,901**	**$178,901**	**0.2218**	**1 year: $36,366** **3 Year: $109,097**
Cause of Injury: Motor Vehicle - NOC						
OK	4/1/2014	1327	$85,338	$85,338	0.0891	1 year: $14,609 3 year: $43,826
OK	4/1/2013	1174	$8,701	$8,701	0.0289	1 year: $4,738 3 year: $14,215
OK	4/1/2014	1342	$4,084	$4,084	0.0136	1 year: $2,230 3 year: $6,689
Subtotals **Number of losses: 3**			**$98,173**	**$98,173**	**0.1316**	**1 year: $21,577** **3 Year: $64,730**
Cause of Injury: Strain / Injury from - Twisting						
OK	4/1/2013	1231	$75,676	$75,676	0.0842	1 year: $13,805 3 year: $41,416
Subtotals **Number of losses: 1**			**$75,676**	**$75,676**	**0.0842**	**1 year: $13,805** **3 Year: $41,416**

Figure 7-4. Homing in on key causes of injury

CHAPTER 8

WORKING WITH CLAIMS

TV ads for personal insurance tell happy stories. Somebody's car is banged up, or a portion of a house is accidentally demolished by a sports-star celebrity appearing in the ad, and almost before a claim can be filed, the insurance adjuster is there with the money.

True stories in commercial insurance often follow a rather different story arc. You spend time putting together a claim, and when you file it, the

Virtually every claim is open to negotiation. And the insured should be ready to question or contest anything that doesn't make sense in the insurance company's handling of a claim.

haggling begins. In order for the claim to work, you have to work it.

This should not be surprising. All insurance is in the form of legal contracts, and contracts are open to interpretation and negotiation. Therefore, virtually every claim is open to negotiation. And the insured should be ready to question or contest anything that doesn't make sense in the insurance company's handling of a claim.

Even in my personal insurance—dealing with insurance companies that I also do business with on the commercial side—I've had to get people involved at upper levels to make sure the claims department handled the claim the way they should have, because they didn't realize that I knew what I was doing.

Here is an example. My daughter was in an auto accident, which was clearly not her fault—her car was hit while it was standing still. Luckily there were no serious injuries, but the car was totaled, so the claim proceeds should have been enough to buy a comparable vehicle in our geographic area. The other driver's insurance company sent me an appraisal that looked very much like a lowball. I called them and said, "Look, I'm finding higher values right on the internet; where did you get your comparables?" They said they got them from dealerships near my home, and they named three that supposedly had a car of that kind. So I took the appraisal, went to one of the dealerships, and said, "I would like to see this vehicle, because I think I'm going to buy it." The man looked at the appraisal and said, "This vehicle does not exist." Next dealership, same thing: "We don't have anything like that on our lot."

So, where did the appraisal come from? You tell me. This insurer had used an independent appraisal company. And what that company did, I suspect, was just call around to dealerships, ask for the used-car person, and say, "Hey, what do you think such-and-such a car is worth?" Then maybe they picked the lowest numbers that people threw at them. You can't do that. You need to have something today that I can buy, to establish the value. You need to have something I can buy because *I need to buy it to replace the thing I lost.*

The situation with the car was urgent enough that I went ahead, found and bought a comparable replacement—at a higher price than the appraisal, of course—and only then resumed dickering with the appraisers to make up the difference.

Nor is this story by any means an outlier. The same thing happened with a claim on a piece of equipment that was stolen from one of my commercial clients. The adjuster sent me an appraisal that left me shaking my head. So I started calling the dealers they supposedly talked to, and I said, "My client needs this particular backhoe. If you have it on your lot, he'll buy it."

"I'm sorry, we don't have anything similar to that on our lot."

"Well, I'm looking at an appraisal that says you have one."

And, as of the time I'm telling this story, we're still working on the claim. There are legitimate complications that can come up with any claim involving replacement of a stolen or damaged vehicle. For one thing, you'll never find an exact duplicate. The mileage or the model year are different; the options are different. With the backhoe, I found a dealer who had a 2009 model. My client's stolen backhoe was a 2006—and the adjuster wanted to deduct an amount from the 2009's price for depreciation.

I argued, correctly I believe, that the model year of a backhoe doesn't matter in the way it does on a used car. A backhoe is a practical thing. You do not care about its appearance or its resale value because you don't intend to impress your neighbors or resell it. You want to keep the backhoe and use it for digging holes for as long as it will do the job to your satisfaction. What counts for that purpose is how many service hours it has accumulated, and the fewer the better. The 2009 had more hours on it than my client's 2006 did when it was stolen! But although I managed to make the point (I think), the adjuster brought up another point of contention, which is why the beat goes on at this time.

SOME LESSONS TO HEED

I have confidence in my ability to work with claims. If the adjuster and I can't come to an agreement, the next step is going up the chain of command at the insurance company, and the next step if that doesn't work is deciding whether it would pay to go to court over the claim. I've learned how to play the game at all of these stages. I have learned the following, among other things.

It's usually best for a client to let someone like me, or my brokerage's on-staff claims professional, try everything we can try in direct negotiation before going to court. It's much cheaper to have your broker/agent carry the ball (or to carry it yourself) than to pay an attorney—and it helps to be able to hold out the option of hiring an attorney and going to court as leverage in the negotiation.

However, claims that progress to the lawsuit stage call for the insurance company adjuster to engage an attorney right away. Typically, they are cases in which you're defending a liability claim against you, as a defendant has a relatively short period of time to file an initial answer to the suit. The insurance company would provide an attorney to defend you against the covered allegations. The catch is, sometimes there could be allegations that aren't covered by insurance. The claimant might allege that not only are you liable for harm done by the accident, you also committed a heinous act of another kind. In this case, you need your own attorney ASAP, as well.

A third lesson, unfortunately, is that aside from a few exceptions, like those mentioned above, there are not many "typicals" you can rely on when you're working with claims. Anything can happen. For instance, I didn't expect to encounter an insurance company appraising a backhoe with the same "precision" as if it were a commonly available Lexus. Each claim is an event that hasn't occurred before. Certainly you can find precedents or parallels to serve as guidelines, but those are open to interpretation, too. It helps to get as clear an understanding of the facts of the situation as possible, and then apply a good dose of common sense.

So, I will wrap up this learning exercise by quoting from someone else's general guidelines for working with claims. The someone else is a recognized and multiple-credentialed authority: Bill Wilson, author of the book *When Words Collide: Resolving Insurance Coverage and Claims Disputes.* In the book, he presents "Doctrines 1–10" to be mindful of. The Wilson Doctrines have been widely quoted in their brief form, as I'm doing here—except, I have added my own interpretation of each one. Along with one "Doctrine" of my own: Doctrine 11.

BILL WILSON'S DOCTRINES

I have listed these doctrines below and provided my fleshed-out explanation of each:

Doctrine 1: *"Insurance is not a commodity."* When you're buying something like personal auto insurance, it's much closer to a commodity because the contracts are pretty standardized. But commercial insurance contracts get tailored and modified with so-called endorsements. The endorsements make each contract unique enough that you can't compare one to another on an apples-to-apples basis. As Wilson says, it's not a commodity.

Doctrine 2: *"RTFC."* In polite language suitable for church, this means "read the full contract." You don't know what you have unless you've read it. If it's seventy-five pages long and full of complexity, as many contracts are, have a competent person read it and explain it.

Doctrine 3: "*Don't accept a claim denial as gospel.*" Just because an insurer denies a claim up front does not mean that's ultimately what is going to happen. The insurer is staking out a position. Of course, if the position is grounded in rock-solid evidence and reasoning, the denial will stand, but I certainly haven't found that to be the case every time.

Doctrine 4: "*The purpose of insurance is to insure.*" That's why you are entering into a contract—in order to be insured. The insurance company has an obligation, at least in theory, to look to try to find coverage for a claim.

Doctrine 5: "*All parties have a duty of utmost good faith.*" Insurance is a purchase of mutual trust, and so, in good faith, the insurance company should be trying to find coverage, and the customer should be telling the truth about the circumstances.

Doctrine 6: "*Most insurance policies are contracts of adhesion, so insuring agreements are interpreted broadly, exclusions narrowly, and ambiguities in favor of the insured.*" This is a mouthful. Let's take it bite by bite. A contract of adhesion is a contract that's been written by one party, and the other party is pretty much stuck with it, as written. Insurance contracts tend to be that way. You can ask for changes, and certainly there will be parts that are tailored to your situation. But you can't ask the insurance company to tear up the policy and write a new one just for you, or to use one that your cousin wrote. Your negotiating power is limited; you are the stuckee.

The rest of the doctrine essentially says that because of this, you are owed a break. Gray areas and tough calls should be decided your way—theoretically. Of course, insurance companies don't always behave theoretically, and the courts, which are the ultimate deciders of what a contract says, can interpret things differently depending on the jurisdiction and many other factors.

Doctrine 7: "*The burden of proof in determining coverage rests with both parties.*" It's up to the client to prove the circumstances. It's up to the insurance company to prove why they're right if they disagree with the client.

Doctrine 8: "*Exclusions must be clear and conspicuous.*" An insurance contract tells you what's covered, and then further on it tells you all the things that aren't covered, which are supposedly spelled out clearly in a section called "Exclusions." But again, they can be somewhat ambiguous, and there can be differing interpretations, so negotiation may come in.

I remember a liability claim I was involved with years ago. My client was boring underground and hit a sewer line that ran from a person's house. Sewage backed up into the house, so my client was clearly liable for the cleanup. But initially the insurance company denied the claim based on a pollution exclusion that clearly didn't apply to this particular situation. The specific exclusion was designed to apply to cases where you pollute the environment with substances that you use or generate in your work. For example, if your chemical storage tank leaks and pollutes the soil or the aquifers in your area, the remediation costs will be high, and they'd be excluded. How this came to be seen as applying to my client's case is a mystery; maybe a new adjuster wanted to be creative. But we got the denial overturned relatively quickly, and the story comes back to the point I made at the start: Every claim is potentially a negotiation.

Doctrine 9: "*The duty to defend is broader than the duty to indemnify.*" In other words, in a third-party claim, the insurer has a duty to defend you against the third party unless there is an extremely good reason not to. You're buying two things in a liability policy:

defense and then indemnification, if you're found to be liable. The defense comes first. People forget this when they think about whether they really need to buy a particular type of liability insurance. The question is not whether you would ever do the thing that the insurance covers; the question is, could somebody ever *say* that you did it? Because if they can accuse you of it and you have to defend yourself, it can be very expensive to prove that you're right.

Doctrine 10: "*Folklore is not fact.*" It doesn't matter what you hear about how something works, or how it supposedly happened, or how it should be. Each claim has a story behind it, full of particular details. These need to be assessed and interpreted in terms of the insurance contract and the case law for that jurisdiction. Ultimately, when a claim goes to court, the court decides what the "facts" are and what the contract says.

> **Claims adjusters and other insurance company people are your fellow humans. You will do best if you treat them as such.**

And now one more, from the author of this book ...

Doctrine 11: *Although they can be contentious—and sometimes seemingly incompetent, as well—claims adjusters and other insurance company people are your fellow humans. You will do best if you treat them as such.*

When a claims dispute turns hopelessly adversarial, you may have no alternative to letting the claws come out. And you certainly need to stand your ground when you believe you are in the right. And yes, some insurance people and companies are better or worse than others, and you're going to have both good and bad experiences with all of them.

But if you are using a good, solid insurance company, you are much more likely to get a fair or positive result by coming in human to human. When I'm going into a potentially adversarial situation, I've had much better luck believing that adjusters are professionals who want to pay what people are entitled to—but they have to answer to bosses, and they get second-guessed and questioned. When I look at it in that way, my role is to help the adjuster build a case for giving my client everything that they are due.

Which goes back to the concept of owning your risk. If you look at yourself as an owner, know that you own the claim, and believe that you have the ammunition that you can give to someone to prove-up the claim, then you have a high likelihood of a good outcome.

CHAPTER 9

IMMEDIATE SAVINGS (AND MORE)

We have done some heavy lifting in this book. We've looked at major steps you can take in managing your risk to make a big difference in the cost. It's time for aerobics. Here are fifty-one simpler things you can do more quickly that might save anywhere from a little to a lot on your insurance premiums. They are broken out into sections for the common foundational insurance lines: workers' compensation, general liability, auto, and property. There's a bonus section of ten general tips at the end.

IMMEDIATE SAVINGS ON WORKERS' COMPENSATION

1. **Review the classification codes for accuracy.** Rates for workers' compensation are based, in part, on the types of work done by people in your company. Construction workers face more risk than office clerks, so you'll be charged more to insure them. Insurance companies have classification

codes for just about every kind of work—from sales to steel erection, painting, plumbing, and more—and at some point, they've had an agent put everyone in your company into what they think is the proper code.

But sometimes the code doesn't match what people really do. If a wrong code carries a higher rate than the right one, and if a lot of people are misclassified in that same way, you could be overpaying significantly—year after year—without knowing it. I have found this happening many times.

Once, looking for new business, I visited a company that makes valves for the oil and gas industries. They had a shop full of people insured under the company's "governing" classification code, which of course was "Valve Manufacturing." But when I walked through their manufacturing facility, I saw *big* valves, with diameters above the range that my experience led me to expect and an order of magnitude bigger than the valves you would find in places like your home water lines. I started to wonder if there were different codes for making different-sized valves. So I did some research, and sure enough, those workers belonged in the "Oil Tool Manufacturing" code. At about *half* the rate. We appealed the classification code to the state workers' compensation commission and got the company's premium cut in half overnight.

Check the classification codes in the ratings section of your policy. It may be worth your time.

2. **For the end-of-year audit in a guaranteed cost plan, make sure the overtime "bonus" is removed from your payroll records.** As we saw in chapter 5, guaranteed cost actually means "guaranteed rate." Your actual cost will be

determined at the end of each year by an audit of your actual risk exposures versus what you projected they would be at the start. This includes the total number of hours worked by your hourly employees—which the auditor checks simply by comparing your final payroll costs to the initial estimate. Suppose a company estimates it will pay $10 million in wages and winds up paying $11.5 million. The workers' comp premium will be increased in proportion to the $1.5 million overrun.

But wait: What if all of it came from overtime work, on which the company paid time and a half? In that case, payroll cost is giving an inflated picture of the actual additional hours worked. And the company is billed for a higher premium surcharge than it should be. *See that overtime bonuses are recorded separately from straight-time pay* in the payroll records you submit for audit. If our hypothetical company had done this, they'd be correctly showing $1 million worth of extra hours worked on a straight-time basis, not $1.5 million, and they would save money on the premium.

3. **Maximize the payroll that you allocate to "standard exception" classification codes.** Auditors are taught to put as much of your payroll as they can into the governing classification code for your type of business. But you're allowed to take out of that governing code what are called standard exception classifications, of which the four primary ones are for clerical staff, sales, executive officers, and drivers. Make sure you get them all. The rates for these codes are very low. (And rates for governing codes are generally much higher.)

4. **See that executive officers' payroll is limited as per state rules, too.** When your top people are put into the classification code for executive officers, you get an extra benefit. Not only is the rate low, there's also a limit on the dollar amount of salary that is entered for each person. A CEO might earn $1 million per year, but if the limit is, say, $65,000 (it varies from state to state), then only $65,000 counts against payroll. And since premium depends on payroll, you save.

5. **Be sure you have certificates of insurance for all subcontractors.** If you use subcontractors, of course you pay them. But you do not want to pay their insurance premiums, which can be mistakenly charged to you unless you receive—from each—a certificate of insurance showing that those subcontractors have their own insurance.

6. **Implement an effective return-to-work program.** It actually pays to get injured workers back on the payroll as soon as possible. This could mean having them do less strenuous work temporarily, but if they can perform useful activity within their doctors' guidelines, here's why it pays. When people are at home collecting workers' comp benefits, those "salary indemnity" payments will count against your experience modifier for the next three years, raising your premium every time. If those same people are on the job, you pay once and get work in return instead of none. A good broker could help you calculate when it's best to do which.

   Workers, too, usually benefit from returning sooner rather than later. As dictated by the workers' comp laws in most states, injured workers receive only about two-thirds of their usual wages. And if they spend time sitting at home watching

TV, they're going to see ads from law firms urging them to sue you, which is unlikely to get them more money than otherwise but creates a less-than-ideal situation for you.

7. **Audit your experience modifier calculations.** As we saw in chapter 7, mistakes can be made.

8. **See that successful subrogation claims are removed from your claims history and your experience rating calculations.** Subrogation occurs when you have workers who are injured, through no fault of theirs or yours, by another party's actions—for example, they're in a work vehicle hit by a reckless driver. Often your insurance company will pay the claim and then go after the responsible party in order to be reimbursed. If they are, the money they receive should not count as part of your losses in any records or calculations.

9. **Consider a deductible, especially in states that exclude deductible payments from the experience modifier calculation.** This is another case where a good broker can help you figure out a course of action most likely to minimize your costs. You might do best by taking a deductible amount that keeps your modifier low and keeps small claims out of your records entirely.

10. **Audit all insurance company audits.** Not doing this is analogous to letting the IRS compute your income tax. As we've seen repeatedly, humans who work for insurance companies can make mistakes, overlook things, or interpret things in a questionable manner. It should not be surprising if errors tend to lean in the insurance company's favor at your expense. Just as you want a CPA doing your taxes in a way that works out fair and square for you, capturing every

possible advantage, it's good to have a knowledgeable person audit your insurance company's audits.

11. **Verify that your workers' comp carrier audits all medical bills and passes along the savings.** You have seen news about US government audits that catch overcharges in Medicare billing. For the same reason, your workers' comp insurer should be auditing the medical bills it pays, and when over-billings are found, the savings should accrue to you at least in part. Some carriers will pass the entire amount to you minus a small audit fee. Others, being less generous, will split the savings with you. Whatever the case, verify that it's done.

12. **Take advantage of premium-reduction programs in your state.** Keep in mind that workers' compensation insurers are governed, in each state, by a board or commission that can have substantial influence on the premiums you pay. Some states offer discounts or reductions of your premium to incentivize what they consider good practices. I have seen programs that reduce your premium by a few percent for meeting drug-free workplace requirements, and ones that offer savings of more than 10 percent for going with a man-aged-care provider. Check for programs currently available in your state.

13. **Have your claims reports set up so that they provide useful, actionable information.** Most insurance carriers now have the ability to let you specify how claims data are broken out and reported to you. This puts a great diagnostic tool in your hands. The right breakouts can reveal patterns that help you focus loss-control efforts on major sources of

loss. For instance, you could ask to see losses reported in the following areas:

- Locations, branches, or departments—Are there key trouble spots, injury-wise?

- Day and time of day—When are accidents most likely?

- Type of injury—What are the most frequent kinds? The most severe and costly?

- Characteristics of injured workers—Are new hires getting hurt? Do they need training in particular skills? Are they being put on risky jobs too soon?

Interesting cross-patterns can emerge. In one case, I saw an unusual frequency of knee injuries that were supposedly incurred on Fridays but were reported to the company on Mondays … by young workers, in an area where weekend soccer games are popular. The data won't tell you what to do but can point to where potential savings lie.

14. **Tie a portion of managers' compensation to the workers' compensation experience in their departments.** A common incentive that may well produce results.

15. **Thoroughly investigate all accidents; document all results; get all statements (plus photos/videos) immediately; learn lessons from each one.** This has twofold benefits: (1) you are fully armed with the ammunition to resolve a claim; and (2) you can learn how to prevent further claims instead of learning how history repeats itself.

16. **Consistently monitor claims to assure they aren't overre-served.** An overreserved claim can cost you money in more

ways than one, and if you're working with an adjuster who has an ongoing tendency to overreserve, the costs add up.

17. **After an injury, keep the injured employee reassured and well informed, by both your company and the insurance company.** When people who've been hurt begin to feel alienated, scared, or uncertain, they become more likely to retain an attorney. Let them know you are on their side. See that the insurance company contacts them to answer any questions about coverage. Claims that turn adversarial are costly. When you and the insurer are reaching out to help an injured worker feel good and get well, everyone wins.

IMMEDIATE SAVINGS ON GENERAL LIABILITY

1. **Review all classification codes.** As with workers' comp, you want a policy in which the codes and rates are right.

2. **Make sure all clerical wages are excluded from the ratings basis.** Clerical staff pose minimal GL risk and shouldn't be factored in when calculating the rates.

3. **Consider liability deductibles and/or self-insured retentions.** The difference between a deductible and a self-insured retention lies in when the insurance company gets involved in the claim. With a deductible, the insured turns the claim over to the insurance company immediately. When it is settled, the insurance company is reimbursed by the insured for the amount of the deductible. With a self-insured retention, the insured handles the claim, to include settlement, up until the retention amount is exceeded. When the retention is

exceeded, it is then that the insured turns the claim over to the insurance company.

Usually, carriers will allow deductibles for either property damage only, bodily injury only, or both combined. I generally don't recommend self-insured retentions for bodily injury. Claims for bodily injuries to third parties can run sky high, and in my judgment it's just better to have the insurance company dealing with them from the very beginning. This logic applies particularly to larger retentions. (With deductibles, there's not much difference one way or the other, as the insurance company handles the claim from the beginning).

4. **Get the benefit of all payroll (including the owners) limitations and exemptions.** This should be self-explanatory.

5. **Make sure intracompany sales are not counted twice.** A company may be set up so that one unit essentially "sells" goods to another unit, which then processes the goods further and sells them to customers. Obviously you wouldn't want both transactions counted into total sales volume for determining your GL premium.

6. **See that overtime charges are excluded from payroll.** This repeats the advice of the second point under workers' comp.

7. **Obtain certificates of insurance from all subcontractors, evidencing their GL coverage.** And this parallels the fifth point under workers' comp.

8. **Consider asking your primary carrier to increase your limit from $1 million to $2 million.** In today's markets, a primary insurance carrier may only offer GL (or auto liability) coverage up to $1 million. An "umbrella" carrier

takes it from there, selling as much additional coverage as you think would be wise, given that liability claims can run well up into the multiple millions. But umbrella rates are going up, too. We have found that in some cases it's cheaper to have the primary carrier write your policy for $2 million, if they're willing, because the incremental charge is less than you would pay for that first additional million from an umbrella carrier.

9. **Ensure that driver payroll is not included in the premium base, unless the governing code includes drivers.** Driver payroll is exempt unless the governing code specifically includes it.

10. **Try to project your payroll and sales for the policy year as realistically as possible—especially on "Excess and Surplus Lines" policies.** In any plan where the actual, total premium is determined by a year-end audit, it's helpful if your initial projections of the basis figures are close to the mark. If you buy insurance in the E&S (excess and surplus) market, it's better to err on the conservative side—that is, projecting payroll and sales a bit lower than they turn out to be, so you wind up owing an additional charge. E&S carriers generally insure types of businesses that are considered too risky by the major "admitted" insurance companies. They are much less likely to grant a credit or refund when the final audit numbers show that you've overpaid.

IMMEDIATE SAVINGS ON COMMERCIAL AUTO INSURANCE

1. **See that each vehicle's "use" classification is accurate— and likewise for garaging location, vehicle weight, and radius of travel.** These are the four main factors that insurers look at to judge risk and therefore the rates they'll charge. A truck used constantly for deliveries has more risk exposure to accidents than one parked most of the day at a job site. Some garaging locations (generally delineated by county) are riskier than others due to amounts of traffic on the area's roads; a big, heavy vehicle can do more damage than a small one and is harder to get stopped; and any vehicle encounters more risk if it's traveling long distances. A simple run-through to check each vehicle's information can turn up errors that yield savings when fixed.

2. **Consider "Specified Causes of Loss" for work vehicles.** Within your auto policy, you have comprehensive and collision coverages. Comprehensive means everything other than collision, such as theft of the vehicle or any other damages it might incur not associated with a collision. For commercial vehicles, there is an alternative called "Specified Causes of Loss." It covers the major risks, including theft, and it's cheaper. The main coverage you lose is windshield glass breakage.

3. **Raise physical damage deductibles.** Just taking, say, a $2,000 deductible instead of $1,000 can save a significant amount on premiums across a fleet of vehicles. And, while you should run an estimate on this, the chances are probably low that the incremental costs of deductible payments would

wipe out the premium savings, especially on later-model (newer) fleets.

4. **Drop physical damage coverage for older vehicles.** At a certain stage in any vehicle's life, you may find it more cost effective to take full responsibility for repairs, deciding which damages are worth fixing and to what extent.

5. **Consider a liability deductible.** Liability is your main risk concern as a business owner, and if you feel confident in your company's safety capabilities, the premium savings from a deductible could outweigh the odds of your having to pay it.

6. **Be sure mobile equipment is not on the auto policy.** You do not need auto insurance for a vehicle that is not licensed for on-the-road use. Bulldozers and other vehicles that are hauled to job sites, or used only within company premises, belong on what's called a "Mobile Equipment" policy.

7. **Develop and enforce a distracted driver program.** Distracted driving is a source of risk that every company needs to confront effectively. Loss concerns are high across the board—in terms of both frequency and severity of accidents and in terms of harm to both the company's people and others. Further, "distractions" aren't limited to using cell phones. Horseplay with passengers and grooming or shaving while driving are among the many behaviors that can be dangerous and costly. A range of preventive measures are available. Your broker or safety professional can help with development of a program, which then needs to be well implemented and strictly enforced. Zero tolerance should be part of the package.

8. **Screen and monitor motor vehicle records (MVRs) for all drivers.** Some businesses assume their insurance agent will do this, but the business itself is responsible. Check the MVRs of every employee who drives *or potentially could drive* a company vehicle and recheck periodically. Most companies with big fleets review MVRs quarterly; once per year should be the minimum. Allowing someone with a poor record to get behind the wheel raises your risk of a costly accident to begin with and makes it very tough to defend against a liability claim.

9. **Conduct rapid and thorough investigations of all accidents; get statements immediately.** As with workplace accidents, there's a twofold purpose. You want to arm yourself with accurate information concerning the claim and learn how to avoid future claims.

10. **Ensure that all drivers are current in defensive-driver training.** If you practice defensive driving, you probably know that it works. It can make the difference between having "only a couple of accidents" on your record and none at all. Training is widely available and could more than pay for itself.

IMMEDIATE SAVINGS ON PROPERTY INSURANCE

1. **Take the maximum deductible that makes sense.** Your company's buildings need to be amply insured, but there is strong potential for savings on the premium. You are very familiar with the property and the uses for which you need it. The risks to the property, and the costs of repairing it

or replacing it in case of loss, are usually more knowable and controllable than when you're dealing with people and liabilities. This knowledge, combined with the amount of credit your insurer offers for deductibles, should equip you to choose the largest deductible that makes financial sense.

2. **Be sure the insurance carrier has accurate "COPE" information on all of your structures.** The carrier will set rates that reflect each facility's

- construction,

- occupancy,

- protection (from mainly fire and wind), and

- exposure (to flood, wind, storms, etc., along with ingress/ egress).

Inaccuracies occur, and details of these factors can change, so it's worth checking.

3. **Consider fire protection systems in places where you don't already have them.** Equipment such as automatic sprinklers can garner some rate credits as well as actually douse fires.

And last, but not least ...

4. **Review business interruption coverages and limits, with particular attention to redundancies or alternate production arrangements.** The worst-case property risk is that essential manufacturing or administrative facilities will be destroyed or rendered unusable. This can happen out of nowhere, and a company must be properly prepared. Business interruption insurance attempts to cover lost revenue and increased expenses from a covered event, but

unfortunately it won't satisfy customers who rely on you and/or your products. The coverage should provide at least a bridge until your operations can be repaired, replaced, or shifted elsewhere. Backup resources could include branch locations, redundant machinery, or agreements to contract out your production to others. A broker's assistance can be crucial in developing a plan sufficient for avoiding a significant business interruption loss and for selecting the proper limits of insurance to purchase.

IN GENERAL ...

1. **Take an active role in all claims.** Make sure the insurance adjuster has all relevant facts and details. Per my advice in chapter 8, a good approach is to treat adjusters as people who want to do right, and give them the ammunition they need to make your case to their superiors. If that fails, your broker can help pursue the claim further.

2. **Consider periodic claims reviews.** This assures that claims won't be overlooked or mishandled. You want to go over them with a representative from the insurance company on a regular basis. Check to see that reserves are proper and that everybody's communicating on every claim. The latter is important for heading off problems in which one party thinks that another party knows or is doing something when in fact they don't or they aren't.

3. **Engage specialized accounting firms to handle business interruption claims.** These are extraordinary events. You should have expertise to match. On behalf of several clients,

I have engaged a firm that's able to provide broad-based services, including forensic accounting, for recovery from emergency and disaster situations.

4. **Don't hesitate to ask for advance payments on property and other first-party claims.** The insurance company can tell pretty quickly whether claims like this have merit. And you may need money quickly to pay for repairs or replacement equipment without tapping a credit line.

5. **Analyze loss reports for accuracy.** Enough said.

6. **If the decision is made to market an account, be prepared and thorough—with all relevant information—and go to market early.** Prospective insurers will want to see your loss history and other data, which should be accurate and reflect you fairly. To find a good match with a good carrier, allow several months' lead time. Last-minute shopping isn't the way to get into an important contract that can affect both your finances and your people.

7. **Consolidate renewal dates to one date.** Then you go through the process only once a year and gain efficiency.

8. **Purchase as many lines as possible from one carrier.** This gives you the maximum bang for your buck, as the carrier has more premiums of yours with which to pay claims. It also protects you in case one line of insurance should have a major claim or claims, as the lines with good experience balance out the line with bad experience.

9. **Don't shop your insurance program too frequently.** Too many people ignore this advice. Perhaps they don't recognize the extent to which insurance is a relationship. It's a rocky

one sometimes, but it is much more of a relationship business than day trading or home-mortgage refinance, where people accept that you will always be chasing the next deal.

Good insurance companies are not interested in accounts that have been shopped a lot. They don't want to write your business this year and have it gone next year over a few dollars' difference. You may save some money on the first hop or two, but over the long run you will pay more. Reliable carriers with good rates and claim service may not even give you a look. And, you will lose your loyalty credits—the advantages, efficiencies, and benefits of the doubt that can come with being a loyal customer of a company that wants to keep you.

Recently one of my clients had an unusually bad claims year. He'd been with the same major insurance company for about ten years. They raised his rates, but not as much as they could have. Another client had a truly horrendous claim. His insurer was about to dump him, which would've put him in a hard place at the worst possible time to be looking for coverage. But we pointed out to the insurer that he'd been a good account for a long time and would probably be an even better account in the future due to the lessons learned from the terrible accident and the motivation of never wanting to have such a claim again. The insurance company kept him, and it has worked out very well.

Now imagine what would happen to either of these two business owners if they were in their first year with the latest of a series of "cheaper" insurance companies. The grass is not always greener. Sometimes the mud just gets deeper.

10. **Use a broker/agent with substantial experience in your industry or with your size account.** This minimizes oversights and helps with efficiencies. It also takes us to the next chapter.

CHAPTER 10

WHAT A BROKER CAN DO

S hould I close this book with an advertisement for my firm and for me? Let me put it this way: I want to inform you what a *good* broker or agent can do for you, which might be different and beyond what you have been conditioned to expect up until now. I consider my team and my firm to be excellent at what we do. If you were to contact us as a result of the information in this chapter, we surely wouldn't mind. But I will also be happy if you can just take advantage of my experience and thoughts on the subject to benefit your current relationship.

So, here is what many business owners and leaders customarily expect from a broker. They see the broker as someone who can find them a good deal on insurance, execute the transaction, and be around when help is needed with something.

In my opinion, this is a limited viewpoint. It sees the broker's role as something like a website you would use for getting good deals on airfares. The website finds and presents options, ranked by cheapest first. It executes the purchase of the one you like. And there's a customer service desk, ready to assist with "renewals" (getting another flight) or with a few common problems that come up.

This viewpoint is widely entrenched. Many brokerages operate on the basis of this model. About 75 percent of their work consists of transactional functions, mainly account placement. The rest of their work is mostly reactive—reacting to customers' normal day-to-day service needs.

If that's all you are looking for, there are plenty of brokers who will provide it. We are not one of them. We have a bigger vision as to what we want to accomplish for our clients. We certainly do the transactional things in what we believe is an excellent manner, but we want to be more than that. We want to proactively help our clients become better businesses—to whatever level they may aspire to, and which for the ambitious hopefully means "**best in class**"—by helping them to better understand their risks and then take strategic ownership of those risks.

> **The closer you can get to best in class in terms of your risk profile, the more attractive you are to the best insurance companies.**

In our experience, clients who take this approach are able to reap the most value, by far, for their companies. So we believe we built our firm to deliver that value. Only about a third of our time is devoted to the transactional work of placing your insurance contracts and handling day-to-day service needs. These functions are very important but not sufficient. Optimum insurance placements, for example, depend on preparation. The closer you can get to **best in class** in terms of your risk profile, the more attractive you are to the best insurance companies. You will know we've done a good job in helping you get to that stage when we have top insurers competing with each other to write policies for you. We've learned through experience that **best-in-class** businesses—regardless of their particular industries—are able to get not only the best rates but also the most liberal coverage terms, *and* they have the most options when it comes to creative risk financing. They are in charge of their own destiny to the greatest extent possible. They have the greatest likelihood of achieving the lowest total cost of risk over the long term.

Therefore, our fundamental goal is to help you raise your risk profile, either to the next level or to the highest level: **best in class.** This involves our unique process, which is as comprehensive as we can make it. Some of its key elements follow.

Partnering with you to develop first the appropriate mindset and then a strategic process to better understand, better control, and thereby better own your company's risks. Together we'll develop an approach that fits your vision, ambitions, and corporate culture. The end result could be to make a calculated, reasonable step into a new level of risk "ownership," or it could be to optimize a guaranteed cost plan—or it could be to create a hybrid plan that incorporates the best of both of these types of plans.

As your trusted advisor, we'd also partner on an as-needed basis with other professionals whom we know and trust. They might be safety consultants, benefits and HR professionals, forensic accounting firms, business continuity advisors, or many others. By doing this, we may be able to *enhance and support* your existing projects or *suggest and develop* new tactics to improve your business processes and help you become comfortable with the idea of owning more risk.

On an ongoing basis, we partner with you to ensure the satisfactory resolution of all your claims. This is one area where "the rubber meets the road." The reason you buy insurance is to get legitimate claims paid promptly, accurately, and fairly. If we don't get this one right, we probably won't be your broker for very long, and a long-term relationship is what we are all about.

In most matters where you need to negotiate with an insurance company, we think an excellent broker should step into the breach with you to try to take on the role of an "equalizer" who can level the playing field as much as possible. This means bringing to the negotiation our knowledge of the specialized ins and outs of insurance. When needed, it would mean referring you to professionals in our network who are experts in the issue(s) at hand. Either way, we try to support you in such a way that your negotiating posture is at least comparable to, if probably never quite equal to, that of the big, billion-dollar insurance companies.

Of course, we're not the only brokers able to do these things. Even the ones that are 75 percent transactional probably try to do some or many of the things we suggest. And there are firms offering a proactive, strategic, comprehensive approach—except their version of it will be different from ours. That's OK. It means you can choose one that's in harmony with your specific situation or with how you like to work.

And by the way—we also try to be selective in choosing our clients. We are not interested in being like the airfare website. If someone calls and asks us to "round up a few quotes" for their business insurance, and that is really all they are looking for, then we will politely decline. We don't believe that a simple "bid-and-quote, lowest-price-wins" process truly benefits clients in either the short term or the long term, because as mentioned earlier in this book, there is really no such thing as an apples-to-apples comparison in the complicated world of commercial risk financing.

Every insurance contract is different, and every relationship is different. It's unlikely that anyone would get exactly the same coverage terms and conditions at a significantly lower rate just by "getting some quotes." Nor can anyone expect lower rates in years ahead if they are having lots of claims. What makes more sense to us is a consistent, day-by-day focus *on lowering and controlling your total cost of risk.* If we can accomplish that, then choosing between competing insurers becomes one small step in a much more strategic, comprehensive process that is designed to put you in control.

A client who believes in this approach is the kind I'm interested in working with. For me, an ideal client will have most, if not all, the following characteristics:

- They are in the construction or manufacturing industries.

- Current insurance premiums range from about $500,000 to $2 million per year.

- Ownership is actively involved in the business.

- Ownership is committed to improving the company's risk profile.

- Ownership is willing to act upon new or better ideas regarding risk.

- Ownership is interested in improving bottom-line profitability.

- Ownership has a long-term, growth mindset.

- Ownership values transparency, accountability, and loyalty.

- Ownership values a synergistic, trusted-advisor relationship.

A VISION FOR THE ROAD AHEAD

In closing, the main messages I would like to emphasize are these:

Change your mindset.
Own your risk.
Think like an owner, not a renter.

I hope this book has helped to transform your thinking about the relationship between risk and your business. And I hope it encourages you to undertake a systematic process that will lead to a prosperous, long-lasting future for your company. If so, you will embark on a scenario that goes basically like the one you've read about in these chapters.

You'll start with a 360-degree comprehensive review to identify and assess all of your risks. Risks and their associated costs are everywhere, and they are constantly changing. By recognizing them and by taking on an ownership mindset that says you're going to manage and control them, I believe you can flip the script. You can take back control that's been ceded to an insurance company and control your own destiny.

As you work to control losses proactively, you get better at preventing accidents instead of paying for them. This protects your people while it drives down the direct and indirect costs of risk across the board. You also have plans in place for dealing with various big risks that are beyond your control or beyond the scope of insurance to finance.

While making progress on these fronts, you become a stronger company overall. Your ability to own and control risk becomes a true competitive advantage. It enables you to compete, grow, serve your customers, and win new business more effectively than ever.

And, as you move along in this process, you will notice your insurance company taking on a new role in your eyes. They're your partner—an indispensable partner for the things they can do—but you no longer see them as some external monolith in charge of your risk.

You're now thinking and acting like they do—like an owner. You are reaping and keeping rewards that they used to enjoy ... such as streams of dollars which used to flow from your company to theirs *but which now stay in yours.*

How's that for a bottom-line impact? Own your risk.